GNU GSS Library

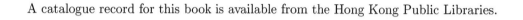

A catalogue record for this book is available from the Hong Kong Public Libraries.

Published in Hong Kong by Samurai Media Limited.

Email: info@samuraimedia.org

ISBN 978-988-8381-66-1

Table of Contents

1 Introduction

GSS is an implementation of the Generic Security Service Application Program Interface (GSS-API). GSS-API is used by network servers to provide security services, e.g., to authenticate SMTP/IMAP clients against SMTP/IMAP servers. GSS consists of a library and a manual.

GSS is developed for the GNU/Linux system, but runs on over 20 platforms including most major Unix platforms and Windows, and many kind of devices including iPAQ handhelds and S/390 mainframes.

GSS is a GNU project, and is licensed under the GNU General Public License version 3 or later.

1.1 Getting Started

This manual documents the GSS programming interface. All functions and data types provided by the library are explained.

The reader is assumed to possess basic familiarity with GSS-API and network programming in C or C++. For general GSS-API information, and some programming examples, there is a guide available online at `http://docs.sun.com/db/doc/816-1331`.

This manual can be used in several ways. If read from the beginning to the end, it gives a good introduction into the library and how it can be used in an application. Forward references are included where necessary. Later on, the manual can be used as a reference manual to get just the information needed about any particular interface of the library. Experienced programmers might want to start looking at the examples at the end of the manual, and then only read up those parts of the interface which are unclear.

1.2 Features

GSS might have a couple of advantages over other libraries doing a similar job.

It's Free Software
>   Anybody can use, modify, and redistribute it under the terms of the GNU General Public License version 3 or later.

It's thread-safe
>   No global variables are used and multiple library handles and session handles may be used in parallell.

It's internationalized
>   It handles non-ASCII names and user visible strings used in the library (e.g., error messages) can be translated into the users' language.

It's portable
>   It should work on all Unix like operating systems, including Windows.

1.3 GSS-API Overview

This section describes GSS-API from a protocol point of view.

The Generic Security Service Application Programming Interface provides security services to calling applications. It allows a communicating application to authenticate the user associated with another application, to delegate rights to another application, and to apply security services such as confidentiality and integrity on a per-message basis.

There are four stages to using the GSS-API:

1. The application acquires a set of credentials with which it may prove its identity to other processes. The application's credentials vouch for its global identity, which may or may not be related to any local username under which it may be running.

2. A pair of communicating applications establish a joint security context using their credentials. The security context is a pair of GSS-API data structures that contain shared state information, which is required in order that per-message security services may be provided. Examples of state that might be shared between applications as part of a security context are cryptographic keys, and message sequence numbers. As part of the establishment of a security context, the context initiator is authenticated to the responder, and may require that the responder is authenticated in turn. The initiator may optionally give the responder the right to initiate further security contexts, acting as an agent or delegate of the initiator. This transfer of rights is termed delegation, and is achieved by creating a set of credentials, similar to those used by the initiating application, but which may be used by the responder.

   To establish and maintain the shared information that makes up the security context, certain GSS-API calls will return a token data structure, which is an opaque data type that may contain cryptographically protected data. The caller of such a GSS-API routine is responsible for transferring the token to the peer application, encapsulated if necessary in an application- application protocol. On receipt of such a token, the peer application should pass it to a corresponding GSS-API routine which will decode the token and extract the information, updating the security context state information accordingly.

3. Per-message services are invoked to apply either: integrity and data origin authentication, or confidentiality, integrity and data origin authentication to application data, which are treated by GSS-API as arbitrary octet-strings. An application transmitting a message that it wishes to protect will call the appropriate GSS-API routine (gss_get_mic or gss_wrap) to apply protection, specifying the appropriate security context, and send the resulting token to the receiving application. The receiver will pass the received token (and, in the case of data protected by gss_get_mic, the accompanying message-data) to the corresponding decoding routine (gss_verify_mic or gss_unwrap) to remove the protection and validate the data.

4. At the completion of a communications session (which may extend across several transport connections), each application calls a GSS-API routine to delete the security context. Multiple contexts may also be used (either successively or simultaneously) within a single communications association, at the option of the applications.

1.4 Supported Platforms

GSS has at some point in time been tested on the following platforms.

1. Debian GNU/Linux 3.0 (Woody)

   GCC 2.95.4 and GNU Make. This is the main development platform. `alphaev67-unknown-linux-gnu`, `alphaev6-unknown-linux-gnu`, `arm-unknown-linux-gnu`, `hppa-unknown-linux-gnu`, `hppa64-unknown-linux-gnu`, `i686-pc-`

`linux-gnu`, `ia64-unknown-linux-gnu`, `m68k-unknown-linux-gnu`, `mips-unknown-linux-gnu`, `mipsel-unknown-linux-gnu`, `powerpc-unknown-linux-gnu`, `s390-ibm-linux-gnu`, `sparc-unknown-linux-gnu`.

2. Debian GNU/Linux 2.1

   GCC 2.95.1 and GNU Make. `armv4l-unknown-linux-gnu`.

3. Tru64 UNIX

   Tru64 UNIX C compiler and Tru64 Make. `alphaev67-dec-osf5.1`, `alphaev68-dec-osf5.1`.

4. SuSE Linux 7.1

   GCC 2.96 and GNU Make. `alphaev6-unknown-linux-gnu`, `alphaev67-unknown-linux-gnu`.

5. SuSE Linux 7.2a

   GCC 3.0 and GNU Make. `ia64-unknown-linux-gnu`.

6. RedHat Linux 7.2

   GCC 2.96 and GNU Make. `alphaev6-unknown-linux-gnu`, `alphaev67-unknown-linux-gnu`, `ia64-unknown-linux-gnu`.

7. RedHat Linux 8.0

   GCC 3.2 and GNU Make. `i686-pc-linux-gnu`.

8. RedHat Advanced Server 2.1

   GCC 2.96 and GNU Make. `i686-pc-linux-gnu`.

9. Slackware Linux 8.0.01

   GCC 2.95.3 and GNU Make. `i686-pc-linux-gnu`.

10. Mandrake Linux 9.0

    GCC 3.2 and GNU Make. `i686-pc-linux-gnu`.

11. IRIX 6.5

    MIPS C compiler, IRIX Make. `mips-sgi-irix6.5`.

12. AIX 4.3.2

    IBM C for AIX compiler, AIX Make. `rs6000-ibm-aix4.3.2.0`.

13. Microsoft Windows 2000 (Cygwin)

    GCC 3.2, GNU make. `i686-pc-cygwin`.

14. HP-UX 11

    HP-UX C compiler and HP Make. `ia64-hp-hpux11.22`, `hppa2.0w-hp-hpux11.11`.

15. SUN Solaris 2.8

    Sun WorkShop Compiler C 6.0 and SUN Make. `sparc-sun-solaris2.8`.

16. NetBSD 1.6

    GCC 2.95.3 and GNU Make. `alpha-unknown-netbsd1.6`, `i386-unknown-netbsdelf1.6`.

17. OpenBSD 3.1 and 3.2

    GCC 2.95.3 and GNU Make. `alpha-unknown-openbsd3.1`, `i386-unknown-openbsd3.1`.

18. FreeBSD 4.7

   GCC 2.95.4 and GNU Make. `alpha-unknown-freebsd4.7`, `i386-unknown-freebsd4.7`.

19. Cross compiled to uClinux/uClibc on Motorola Coldfire.

   GCC 3.4 and GNU Make `m68k-uclinux-elf`.

   If you use GSS on, or port GSS to, a new platform please report it to the author.

1.5 Commercial Support

Commercial support is available for users of GNU GSS. The kind of support that can be purchased may include:

- Implement new features. Such as a new GSS-API mechanism.
- Port GSS to new platforms. This could include porting to an embedded platforms that may need memory or size optimization.
- Integrating GSS as a security environment in your existing project.
- System design of components related to GSS-API.

   If you are interested, please write to:

```
Simon Josefsson Datakonsult AB
Hagagatan 24
113 47 Stockholm
Sweden


E-mail: simon@josefsson.org
```

   If your company provides support related to GNU GSS and would like to be mentioned here, contact the author (see Section 1.7 [Bug Reports], page 5).

1.6 Downloading and Installing

The package can be downloaded from several places, including:

   `ftp://ftp.gnu.org/gnu/gss/`

   The latest version is stored in a file, e.g., 'gss-1.0.3.tar.gz' where the '1.0.3' indicate the highest version number.

   The package is then extracted, configured and built like many other packages that use Autoconf. For detailed information on configuring and building it, refer to the INSTALL file that is part of the distribution archive.

   Here is an example terminal session that downloads, configures, builds and installs the package. You will need a few basic tools, such as 'sh', 'make' and 'cc'.

```
$ wget -q ftp://ftp.gnu.org/gnu/gss/gss-1.0.3.tar.gz
$ tar xfz gss-1.0.3.tar.gz
$ cd gss-1.0.3/
$ ./configure
...
$ make
...
```

```
$ make install
...
```

After that GSS should be properly installed and ready for use.

1.7 Bug Reports

If you think you have found a bug in GSS, please investigate it and report it.

- Please make sure that the bug is really in GSS, and preferably also check that it hasn't already been fixed in the latest version.
- You have to send us a test case that makes it possible for us to reproduce the bug.
- You also have to explain what is wrong; if you get a crash, or if the results printed are not good and in that case, in what way. Make sure that the bug report includes all information you would need to fix this kind of bug for someone else.

Please make an effort to produce a self-contained report, with something definite that can be tested or debugged. Vague queries or piecemeal messages are difficult to act on and don't help the development effort.

If your bug report is good, we will do our best to help you to get a corrected version of the software; if the bug report is poor, we won't do anything about it (apart from asking you to send better bug reports).

If you think something in this manual is unclear, or downright incorrect, or if the language needs to be improved, please also send a note.

Send your bug report to:

'bug-gss@gnu.org'

1.8 Contributing

If you want to submit a patch for inclusion – from solve a typo you discovered, up to adding support for a new feature – you should submit it as a bug report (see Section 1.7 [Bug Reports], page 5). There are some things that you can do to increase the chances for it to be included in the official package.

Unless your patch is very small (say, under 10 lines) we require that you assign the copyright of your work to the Free Software Foundation. This is to protect the freedom of the project. If you have not already signed papers, we will send you the necessary information when you submit your contribution.

For contributions that doesn't consist of actual programming code, the only guidelines are common sense. Use it.

For code contributions, a number of style guides will help you:

- Coding Style. Follow the GNU Standards document (see Section "top" in standards).
  If you normally code using another coding standard, there is no problem, but you should use 'indent' to reformat the code (see Section "top" in indent) before submitting your work.
- Use the unified diff format 'diff -u'.
- Return errors. No reason whatsoever should abort the execution of the library. Even memory allocation errors, e.g. when malloc return NULL, should work although result in an error code.

- Design with thread safety in mind. Don't use global variables. Don't even write to per-handle global variables unless the documented behaviour of the function you write is to write to the per-handle global variable.

- Avoid using the C math library. It causes problems for embedded implementations, and in most situations it is very easy to avoid using it.

- Document your functions. Use comments before each function headers, that, if properly formatted, are extracted into Texinfo manuals and GTK-DOC web pages.

- Supply a ChangeLog and NEWS entries, where appropriate.

1.9 Planned Features

This is also known as the "todo list". If you like to start working on anything, please let me know so work duplication can be avoided.

- Support non-blocking mode. This would be an API extension. It could work by forking a process and interface to it, or by using a user-specific daemon. E.g., h = START(accept_sec_context(...)), FINISHED(h), ret = FINISH(h), ABORT(h).

- Support loadable modules via dlopen, a'la Solaris GSS.

- Port to Cyclone? CCured?

2 Preparation

To use GSS, you have to perform some changes to your sources and the build system. The necessary changes are small and explained in the following sections. At the end of this chapter, it is described how the library is initialized, and how the requirements of the library are verified.

A faster way to find out how to adapt your application for use with GSS may be to look at the examples at the end of this manual.

2.1 Header

All standard interfaces (data types and functions) of the official GSS API are defined in the header file **gss/api.h**. The file is taken verbatim from the RFC (after correcting a few typos) where it is known as **gssapi.h**. However, to be able to co-exist gracefully with other GSS-API implementation, the name **gssapi.h** was changed.

The header file **gss.h** includes **gss/api.h**, and declares a few non-standard extensions (by including **gss/ext.h**), takes care of including header files related to all supported mechanisms (e.g., **gss/krb5.h**) and finally adds C++ namespace protection of all definitions. Therefore, including **gss.h** in your project is recommended over **gss/api.h**. If using **gss.h** instead of **gss/api.h** causes problems, it should be regarded a bug.

You must include either file in all programs using the library, either directly or through some other header file, like this:

```
#include <gss.h>
```

The name space of GSS is **gss_*** for function names, **gss_*** for data types and **GSS_*** for other symbols. In addition the same name prefixes with one prepended underscore are reserved for internal use and should never be used by an application.

Each supported GSS mechanism may want to expose mechanism specific functionality, and can do so through one or more header files under the **gss/** directory. The Kerberos 5 mechanism uses the file **gss/krb5.h**, but again, it is included (with C++ namespace fixes) from **gss.h**.

2.2 Initialization

GSS does not need to be initialized before it can be used.

In order to take advantage of the internationalisation features in GSS, e.g. translated error messages, the application must set the current locale using **setlocale()** before calling, e.g., **gss_display_status()**. This is typically done in **main()** as in the following example.

```
#include <gss.h>
#include <locale.h>
...
  setlocale (LC_ALL, "");
```

2.3 Version Check

It is often desirable to check that the version of GSS used is indeed one which fits all requirements. Even with binary compatibility new features may have been introduced but due to problem with the dynamic linker an old version is actually used. So you may want to check that the version is okay right after program startup. The function is called **gss_check_version()** and is described formally in See Chapter 4 [Extended GSS API], page 57.

The normal way to use the function is to put something similar to the following early in your **main()**:

```
#include <gss.h>

...

  if (!gss_check_version (GSS_VERSION))
    {
      printf ("gss_check_version() failed:\n"
              "Header file incompatible with shared library.\n");
      exit(EXIT_FAILURE);
    }
```

2.4 Building the source

If you want to compile a source file that includes the **gss.h** header file, you must make sure that the compiler can find it in the directory hierarchy. This is accomplished by adding the path to the directory in which the header file is located to the compilers include file search path (via the **-I** option).

However, the path to the include file is determined at the time the source is configured. To solve this problem, GSS uses the external package **pkg-config** that knows the path to the include file and other configuration options. The options that need to be added to the compiler invocation at compile time are output by the **--cflags** option to **pkg-config gss**. The following example shows how it can be used at the command line:

```
gcc -c foo.c `pkg-config gss --cflags`
```

Adding the output of '**pkg-config gss --cflags**' to the compilers command line will ensure that the compiler can find the **gss.h** header file.

A similar problem occurs when linking the program with the library. Again, the compiler has to find the library files. For this to work, the path to the library files has to be added to the library search path (via the **-L** option). For this, the option **--libs** to **pkg-config gss** can be used. For convenience, this option also outputs all other options that are required to link the program with the GSS libarary (for instance, the '**-lshishi**' option). The example shows how to link **foo.o** with GSS into a program **foo**.

```
gcc -o foo foo.o `pkg-config gss --libs`
```

Of course you can also combine both examples to a single command by specifying both options to **pkg-config**:

```
gcc -o foo foo.c `pkg-config gss --cflags --libs`
```

2.5 Out of Memory handling

The GSS API does not have a standard error code for the out of memory error condition. This library will return **GSS_S_FAILURE** and set **minor_status** to ENOMEM.

3 Standard GSS API

3.1 Simple Data Types

The following conventions are used by the GSS-API C-language bindings:

3.1.1 Integer types

GSS-API uses the following integer data type:

    OM_uint32   32-bit unsigned integer

3.1.2 String and similar data

Many of the GSS-API routines take arguments and return values that describe contiguous octet-strings. All such data is passed between the GSS-API and the caller using the `gss_buffer_t` data type. This data type is a pointer to a buffer descriptor, which consists of a length field that contains the total number of bytes in the datum, and a value field which contains a pointer to the actual datum:

```
typedef struct gss_buffer_desc_struct {
    size_t    length;
    void      *value;
} gss_buffer_desc, *gss_buffer_t;
```

Storage for data returned to the application by a GSS-API routine using the `gss_buffer_t` conventions is allocated by the GSS-API routine. The application may free this storage by invoking the `gss_release_buffer` routine. Allocation of the `gss_buffer_desc` object is always the responsibility of the application; unused `gss_buffer_desc` objects may be initialized to the value `GSS_C_EMPTY_BUFFER`.

3.1.2.1 Opaque data types

Certain multiple-word data items are considered opaque data types at the GSS-API, because their internal structure has no significance either to the GSS-API or to the caller. Examples of such opaque data types are the input_token parameter to `gss_init_sec_context` (which is opaque to the caller), and the input_message parameter to `gss_wrap` (which is opaque to the GSS-API). Opaque data is passed between the GSS-API and the application using the `gss_buffer_t` datatype.

3.1.2.2 Character strings

Certain multiple-word data items may be regarded as simple ISO Latin-1 character strings. Examples are the printable strings passed to `gss_import_name` via the input_name_buffer parameter. Some GSS-API routines also return character strings. All such character strings are passed between the application and the GSS-API implementation using the `gss_buffer_t` datatype, which is a pointer to a `gss_buffer_desc` object.

When a `gss_buffer_desc` object describes a printable string, the length field of the `gss_buffer_desc` should only count printable characters within the string. In particular, a trailing NUL character should NOT be included in the length count, nor should either the GSS-API implementation or the application assume the presence of an uncounted trailing NUL.

3.1.3 Object Identifiers

Certain GSS-API procedures take parameters of the type `gss_OID`, or Object identifier. This is a type containing ISO-defined tree- structured values, and is used by the GSS-API caller to select an underlying security mechanism and to specify namespaces. A value of type `gss_OID` has the following structure:

```
typedef struct gss_OID_desc_struct {
   OM_uint32    length;
   void         *elements;
} gss_OID_desc, *gss_OID;
```

The elements field of this structure points to the first byte of an octet string containing the ASN.1 BER encoding of the value portion of the normal BER TLV encoding of the `gss_OID`. The length field contains the number of bytes in this value. For example, the `gss_OID` value corresponding to `iso(1) identified-organization(3) icd-ecma(12) member-company(2) dec(1011) cryptoAlgorithms(7) DASS(5)`, meaning the DASS X.509 authentication mechanism, has a length field of 7 and an elements field pointing to seven octets containing the following octal values: 53,14,2,207,163,7,5. GSS-API implementations should provide constant `gss_OID` values to allow applications to request any supported mechanism, although applications are encouraged on portability grounds to accept the default mechanism. `gss_OID` values should also be provided to allow applications to specify particular name types (see section 3.10). Applications should treat `gss_OID_desc` values returned by GSS-API routines as read-only. In particular, the application should not attempt to deallocate them with free().

3.1.4 Object Identifier Sets

Certain GSS-API procedures take parameters of the type `gss_OID_set`. This type represents one or more object identifiers (see [Object Identifiers], page 10). A `gss_OID_set` object has the following structure:

```
typedef struct gss_OID_set_desc_struct {
   size_t    count;
   gss_OID   elements;
} gss_OID_set_desc, *gss_OID_set;
```

The count field contains the number of OIDs within the set. The elements field is a pointer to an array of `gss_OID_desc` objects, each of which describes a single OID. `gss_OID_set` values are used to name the available mechanisms supported by the GSS-API, to request the use of specific mechanisms, and to indicate which mechanisms a given credential supports.

All OID sets returned to the application by GSS-API are dynamic objects (the `gss_OID_set_desc`, the "elements" array of the set, and the "elements" array of each member OID are all dynamically allocated), and this storage must be deallocated by the application using the `gss_release_oid_set` routine.

3.2 Complex Data Types

3.2.1 Credentials

A credential handle is a caller-opaque atomic datum that identifies a GSS-API credential data structure. It is represented by the caller- opaque type `gss_cred_id_t`.

GSS-API credentials can contain mechanism-specific principal authentication data for multiple mechanisms. A GSS-API credential is composed of a set of credential-elements, each of which is applicable to a single mechanism. A credential may contain at most one credential-element for each supported mechanism. A credential-element identifies the data needed by a single mechanism to authenticate a single principal, and conceptually contains two credential-references that describe the actual mechanism-specific authentication data, one to be used by GSS-API for initiating contexts, and one to be used for accepting contexts. For mechanisms that do not distinguish between acceptor and initiator credentials, both references would point to the same underlying mechanism-specific authentication data.

Credentials describe a set of mechanism-specific principals, and give their holder the ability to act as any of those principals. All principal identities asserted by a single GSS-API credential should belong to the same entity, although enforcement of this property is an implementation-specific matter. The GSS-API does not make the actual credentials available to applications; instead a credential handle is used to identify a particular credential, held internally by GSS-API. The combination of GSS-API credential handle and mechanism identifies the principal whose identity will be asserted by the credential when used with that mechanism.

The `gss_init_sec_context` and `gss_accept_sec_context` routines allow the value `GSS_C_NO_CREDENTIAL` to be specified as their credential handle parameter. This special credential-handle indicates a desire by the application to act as a default principal.

3.2.2 Contexts

The `gss_ctx_id_t` data type contains a caller-opaque atomic value that identifies one end of a GSS-API security context.

The security context holds state information about each end of a peer communication, including cryptographic state information.

3.2.3 Authentication tokens

A token is a caller-opaque type that GSS-API uses to maintain synchronization between the context data structures at each end of a GSS-API security context. The token is a cryptographically protected octet-string, generated by the underlying mechanism at one end of a GSS-API security context for use by the peer mechanism at the other end. Encapsulation (if required) and transfer of the token are the responsibility of the peer applications. A token is passed between the GSS-API and the application using the `gss_buffer_t` conventions.

3.2.4 Interprocess tokens

Certain GSS-API routines are intended to transfer data between processes in multi-process programs. These routines use a caller-opaque octet-string, generated by the GSS-API in one process for use by the GSS-API in another process. The calling application is responsible for transferring such tokens between processes in an OS-specific manner. Note that, while GSS-API implementors are encouraged to avoid placing sensitive information within interprocess tokens, or to cryptographically protect them, many implementations will be unable to avoid placing key material or other sensitive data within them. It is the application's responsibility to ensure that interprocess tokens are protected in transit, and transferred only to processes that are trustworthy. An interprocess token is passed between the GSS-API and the application using the `gss_buffer_t` conventions.

3.2.5 Names

A name is used to identify a person or entity. GSS-API authenticates the relationship between a name and the entity claiming the name.

Since different authentication mechanisms may employ different namespaces for identifying their principals, GSSAPI's naming support is necessarily complex in multi-mechanism environments (or even in some single-mechanism environments where the underlying mechanism supports multiple namespaces).

Two distinct representations are defined for names:

- An internal form. This is the GSS-API "native" format for names, represented by the implementation-specific `gss_name_t` type. It is opaque to GSS-API callers. A single `gss_name_t` object may contain multiple names from different namespaces, but all names should refer to the same entity. An example of such an internal name would be the name returned from a call to the `gss_inquire_cred` routine, when applied to a credential containing credential elements for multiple authentication mechanisms employing different namespaces. This `gss_name_t` object will contain a distinct name for the entity for each authentication mechanism.

  For GSS-API implementations supporting multiple namespaces, objects of type `gss_name_t` must contain sufficient information to determine the namespace to which each primitive name belongs.

- Mechanism-specific contiguous octet-string forms. A format capable of containing a single name (from a single namespace). Contiguous string names are always accompanied by an object identifier specifying the namespace to which the name belongs, and their format is dependent on the authentication mechanism that employs the name. Many, but not all, contiguous string names will be printable, and may therefore be used by GSS-API applications for communication with their users.

Routines (`gss_import_name` and `gss_display_name`) are provided to convert names between contiguous string representations and the internal `gss_name_t` type. `gss_import_name` may support multiple syntaxes for each supported namespace, allowing users the freedom to choose a preferred name representation. `gss_display_name` should use an implementation-chosen printable syntax for each supported name-type.

If an application calls `gss_display_name`, passing the internal name resulting from a call to `gss_import_name`, there is no guarantee the resulting contiguous string name will be the same as the original imported string name. Nor do name-space identifiers necessarily survive unchanged after a journey through the internal name-form. An example of this might be a mechanism that authenticates X.500 names, but provides an algorithmic mapping of Internet DNS names into X.500. That mechanism's implementation of `gss_import_name` might, when presented with a DNS name, generate an internal name that contained both the original DNS name and the equivalent X.500 name. Alternatively, it might only store the X.500 name. In the latter case, `gss_display_name` would most likely generate a printable X.500 name, rather than the original DNS name.

The process of authentication delivers to the context acceptor an internal name. Since this name has been authenticated by a single mechanism, it contains only a single name (even if the internal name presented by the context initiator to `gss_init_sec_context` had multiple components). Such names are termed internal mechanism names, or "MN"s and the names emitted by `gss_accept_sec_context` are always of this type. Since some applications may require MNs without wanting to incur the overhead of an authentication operation, a second function, `gss_canonicalize_name`, is provided to convert a general internal name into an MN.

Comparison of internal-form names may be accomplished via the `gss_compare_name` routine, which returns true if the two names being compared refer to the same entity. This removes the need for the application program to understand the syntaxes of the various printable names that a given GSS-API implementation may support. Since GSS-API assumes that all primitive names contained within a given internal name refer to the same entity, `gss_compare_name` can return true if the two names have at least one primitive name in common. If the implementation embodies knowledge of equivalence relationships between names taken from different namespaces, this knowledge may also allow successful comparison of internal names containing no overlapping primitive elements.

When used in large access control lists, the overhead of invoking `gss_import_name` and `gss_compare_name` on each name from the ACL may be prohibitive. As an alternative way of supporting this case, GSS-API defines a special form of the contiguous string name which may be compared directly (e.g. with memcmp()). Contiguous names suitable for comparison are generated by the `gss_export_name` routine, which requires an MN as input. Exported names may be re- imported by the `gss_import_name` routine, and the resulting internal name will also be an MN. The `gss_OID` constant `GSS_C_NT_EXPORT_NAME` indentifies the "export name" type, and the value of this constant is given in Appendix A. Structurally, an exported name object consists of a header containing an OID identifying the mechanism that authenticated the name, and a trailer containing the name itself, where the syntax of the trailer is defined by the individual mechanism specification. The precise format of an export name is defined in the language-independent GSS-API specification [GSSAPI].

Note that the results obtained by using `gss_compare_name` will in general be different from those obtained by invoking `gss_canonicalize_name` and `gss_export_name`, and then comparing the exported names. The first series of operation determines whether two (unauthenticated) names identify the same principal; the second whether a particular mechanism would authenticate them as the same principal. These two operations will in general give the same results only for MNs.

The `gss_name_t` datatype should be implemented as a pointer type. To allow the compiler to aid the application programmer by performing type-checking, the use of (void *) is discouraged. A pointer to an implementation-defined type is the preferred choice.

Storage is allocated by routines that return `gss_name_t` values. A procedure, `gss_release_name`, is provided to free storage associated with an internal-form name.

3.2.6 Channel Bindings

GSS-API supports the use of user-specified tags to identify a given context to the peer application. These tags are intended to be used to identify the particular communications channel that carries the context. Channel bindings are communicated to the GSS-API using the following structure:

```
typedef struct gss_channel_bindings_struct {
   OM_uint32        initiator_addrtype;
   gss_buffer_desc initiator_address;
   OM_uint32        acceptor_addrtype;
   gss_buffer_desc acceptor_address;
   gss_buffer_desc application_data;
} *gss_channel_bindings_t;
```

The initiator_addrtype and acceptor_addrtype fields denote the type of addresses contained in the initiator_address and acceptor_address buffers. The address type should be one of the following:

```
GSS_C_AF_UNSPEC      Unspecified address type
GSS_C_AF_LOCAL       Host-local address type
GSS_C_AF_INET        Internet address type (e.g. IP)
GSS_C_AF_IMPLINK     ARPAnet IMP address type
GSS_C_AF_PUP         pup protocols (eg BSP) address type
GSS_C_AF_CHAOS       MIT CHAOS protocol address type
GSS_C_AF_NS          XEROX NS address type
GSS_C_AF_NBS         nbs address type
GSS_C_AF_ECMA        ECMA address type
GSS_C_AF_DATAKIT     datakit protocols address type
GSS_C_AF_CCITT       CCITT protocols
GSS_C_AF_SNA         IBM SNA address type
GSS_C_AF_DECnet      DECnet address type
GSS_C_AF_DLI         Direct data link interface address type
GSS_C_AF_LAT         LAT address type
GSS_C_AF_HYLINK      NSC Hyperchannel address type
GSS_C_AF_APPLETALK   AppleTalk address type
GSS_C_AF_BSC         BISYNC 2780/3780 address type
GSS_C_AF_DSS         Distributed system services address type
GSS_C_AF_OSI         OSI TP4 address type
GSS_C_AF_X25         X.25
GSS_C_AF_NULLADDR    No address specified
```

Note that these symbols name address families rather than specific addressing formats. For address families that contain several alternative address forms, the initiator_address and acceptor_address fields must contain sufficient information to determine which address form is used. When not otherwise specified, addresses should be specified in network byte-order (that is, native byte-ordering for the address family).

Conceptually, the GSS-API concatenates the initiator_addrtype, initiator_address, acceptor_addrtype, acceptor_address and application_data to form an octet string. The mechanism calculates a MIC over this octet string, and binds the MIC to the context establishment token emitted by **gss_init_sec_context**. The same bindings are presented by the context acceptor to **gss_accept_sec_context**, and a MIC is calculated in the same way. The calculated MIC is compared with that found in the token, and if the MICs differ, **gss_accept_sec_context** will return a GSS_S_BAD_BINDINGS error, and the context will not be established. Some mechanisms may include the actual channel binding data in the token (rather than just a MIC); applications should therefore not use confidential data as channel-binding components.

Individual mechanisms may impose additional constraints on addresses and address types that may appear in channel bindings. For example, a mechanism may verify that the initiator_address field of the channel bindings presented to `gss_init_sec_context` contains the correct network address of the host system. Portable applications should therefore ensure that they either provide correct information for the address fields, or omit addressing information, specifying `GSS_C_AF_NULLADDR` as the address-types.

3.3 Optional Parameters

Various parameters are described as optional. This means that they follow a convention whereby a default value may be requested. The following conventions are used for omitted parameters. These conventions apply only to those parameters that are explicitly documented as optional.

- gss_buffer_t types. Specify GSS_C_NO_BUFFER as a value. For an input parameter this signifies that default behavior is requested, while for an output parameter it indicates that the information that would be returned via the parameter is not required by the application.
- Integer types (input). Individual parameter documentation lists values to be used to indicate default actions.
- Integer types (output). Specify NULL as the value for the pointer.
- Pointer types. Specify NULL as the value.
- Object IDs. Specify GSS_C_NO_OID as the value.
- Object ID Sets. Specify GSS_C_NO_OID_SET as the value.
- Channel Bindings. Specify GSS_C_NO_CHANNEL_BINDINGS to indicate that channel bindings are not to be used.

3.4 Error Handling

Every GSS-API routine returns two distinct values to report status information to the caller: GSS status codes and Mechanism status codes.

3.4.1 GSS status codes

GSS-API routines return GSS status codes as their `OM_uint32` function value. These codes indicate errors that are independent of the underlying mechanism(s) used to provide the security service. The errors that can be indicated via a GSS status code are either generic API routine errors (errors that are defined in the GSS-API specification) or calling errors (errors that are specific to these language bindings).

A GSS status code can indicate a single fatal generic API error from the routine and a single calling error. In addition, supplementary status information may be indicated via the setting of bits in the supplementary info field of a GSS status code.

These errors are encoded into the 32-bit GSS status code as follows:

```
MSB                                                                       LSB
|-----------------------------------------------------------------------|
```

```
| Calling Error | Routine Error |   Supplementary Info   |
|-------------------------------------------------------|
Bit 31          24 23           16 15                   0
```

Hence if a GSS-API routine returns a GSS status code whose upper 16 bits contain a non-zero value, the call failed. If the calling error field is non-zero, the invoking application's call of the routine was erroneous. Calling errors are defined in table 3-1. If the routine error field is non-zero, the routine failed for one of the routine- specific reasons listed below in table 3-2. Whether or not the upper 16 bits indicate a failure or a success, the routine may indicate additional information by setting bits in the supplementary info field of the status code. The meaning of individual bits is listed below in table 3-3.

Table 3-1 Calling Errors

Name	Value in field	Meaning
GSS_S_CALL_INACCESSIBLE_READ	1	A required input parameter could not be read
GSS_S_CALL_INACCESSIBLE_WRITE	2	A required output parameter could not be written.
GSS_S_CALL_BAD_STRUCTURE	3	A parameter was malformed

Table 3-2 Routine Errors

Name	Value in field	Meaning
GSS_S_BAD_MECH	1	An unsupported mechanism was requested
GSS_S_BAD_NAME	2	An invalid name was supplied
GSS_S_BAD_NAMETYPE	3	A supplied name was of an unsupported type
GSS_S_BAD_BINDINGS	4	Incorrect channel bindings were supplied
GSS_S_BAD_STATUS	5	An invalid status code was supplied
GSS_S_BAD_MIC GSS_S_BAD_SIG	6	A token had an invalid MIC
GSS_S_NO_CRED	7	No credentials were supplied, or the credentials were unavailable or inaccessible.
GSS_S_NO_CONTEXT	8	No context has been established
GSS_S_DEFECTIVE_TOKEN	9	A token was invalid
GSS_S_DEFECTIVE_CREDENTIAL	10	A credential was invalid
GSS_S_CREDENTIALS_EXPIRED	11	The referenced credentials have expired
GSS_S_CONTEXT_EXPIRED	12	The context has expired

GSS_S_FAILURE	13	Miscellaneous failure (see text)
GSS_S_BAD_QOP	14	The quality-of-protection requested could not be provided
GSS_S_UNAUTHORIZED	15	The operation is forbidden by local security policy
GSS_S_UNAVAILABLE	16	The operation or option is unavailable
GSS_S_DUPLICATE_ELEMENT	17	The requested credential element already exists
GSS_S_NAME_NOT_MN	18	The provided name was not a mechanism name

Table 3-3 Supplementary Status Bits

Name	Bit Number	Meaning
GSS_S_CONTINUE_NEEDED	0 (LSB)	Returned only by gss_init_sec_context or gss_accept_sec_context. The routine must be called again to complete its function. See routine documentation for detailed description
GSS_S_DUPLICATE_TOKEN	1	The token was a duplicate of an earlier token
GSS_S_OLD_TOKEN	2	The token's validity period has expired
GSS_S_UNSEQ_TOKEN	3	A later token has already been processed
GSS_S_GAP_TOKEN	4	An expected per-message token was not received

The routine documentation also uses the name GSS_S_COMPLETE, which is a zero value, to indicate an absence of any API errors or supplementary information bits.

All GSS_S_xxx symbols equate to complete OM_uint32 status codes, rather than to bitfield values. For example, the actual value of the symbol GSS_S_BAD_NAMETYPE (value 3 in the routine error field) is 3<<16. The macros GSS_CALLING_ERROR, GSS_ROUTINE_ERROR and GSS_SUPPLEMENTARY_INFO are provided, each of which takes a GSS status code and removes all but the relevant field. For example, the value obtained by applying GSS_ROUTINE_ERROR to a status code removes the calling errors and supplementary info fields, leaving only the routine errors field. The values delivered by these macros may be directly compared with a GSS_S_xxx symbol of the appropriate type. The macro GSS_ERROR is also provided, which when applied to a GSS status code returns a non-zero value if the status code indicated a calling or routine error, and a zero value otherwise. All macros defined by GSS-API evaluate their argument(s) exactly once.

A GSS-API implementation may choose to signal calling errors in a platform-specific manner instead of, or in addition to the routine value; routine errors and supplementary info should be returned via major status values only.

The GSS major status code `GSS_S_FAILURE` is used to indicate that the underlying mechanism detected an error for which no specific GSS status code is defined. The mechanism-specific status code will provide more details about the error.

In addition to the explicit major status codes for each API function, the code `GSS_S_FAILURE` may be returned by any routine, indicating an implementation-specific or mechanism-specific error condition, further details of which are reported via the `minor_status` parameter.

3.4.2 Mechanism-specific status codes

GSS-API routines return a minor_status parameter, which is used to indicate specialized errors from the underlying security mechanism. This parameter may contain a single mechanism-specific error, indicated by a `OM_uint32` value.

The minor_status parameter will always be set by a GSS-API routine, even if it returns a calling error or one of the generic API errors indicated above as fatal, although most other output parameters may remain unset in such cases. However, output parameters that are expected to return pointers to storage allocated by a routine must always be set by the routine, even in the event of an error, although in such cases the GSS-API routine may elect to set the returned parameter value to NULL to indicate that no storage was actually allocated. Any length field associated with such pointers (as in a `gss_buffer_desc` structure) should also be set to zero in such cases.

3.5 Credential Management

```
GSS-API Credential-management Routines


Routine                        Function
-------                        --------

gss_acquire_cred               Assume a global identity; Obtain
                               a GSS-API credential handle for
                               pre-existing credentials.
gss_add_cred                   Construct credentials
                               incrementally.
gss_inquire_cred               Obtain information about a
                               credential.
gss_inquire_cred_by_mech       Obtain per-mechanism information
                               about a credential.
gss_release_cred               Discard a credential handle.
```

gss_acquire_cred

OM_uint32 gss_acquire_cred (*OM_uint32* * minor_status, *const*			[Function]
	gss_name_t desired_name, *OM_uint32* time_req, *const gss_OID_set*
	desired_mechs, *gss_cred_usage_t* cred_usage, *gss_cred_id_t* *
	output_cred_handle, *gss_OID_set* * actual_mechs, *OM_uint32* *
	time_rec)

minor_status: (integer, modify) Mechanism specific status code.

desired_name: (gss_name_t, read) Name of principal whose credential should be acquired.

time_req: (Integer, read, optional) Number of seconds that credentials should remain valid. Specify GSS_C_INDEFINITE to request that the credentials have the maximum permitted lifetime.

desired_mechs: (Set of Object IDs, read, optional) Set of underlying security mechanisms that may be used. GSS_C_NO_OID_SET may be used to obtain an implementation-specific default.

cred_usage: (gss_cred_usage_t, read) GSS_C_BOTH - Credentials may be used either to initiate or accept security contexts. GSS_C_INITIATE - Credentials will only be used to initiate security contexts. GSS_C_ACCEPT - Credentials will only be used to accept security contexts.

output_cred_handle: (gss_cred_id_t, modify) The returned credential handle. Resources associated with this credential handle must be released by the application after use with a call to gss_release_cred().

actual_mechs: (Set of Object IDs, modify, optional) The set of mechanisms for which the credential is valid. Storage associated with the returned OID-set must be released by the application after use with a call to gss_release_oid_set(). Specify NULL if not required.

time_rec: (Integer, modify, optional) Actual number of seconds for which the returned credentials will remain valid. If the implementation does not support expiration of credentials, the value GSS_C_INDEFINITE will be returned. Specify NULL if not required.

Allows an application to acquire a handle for a pre-existing credential by name. GSS-API implementations must impose a local access-control policy on callers of this routine to prevent unauthorized callers from acquiring credentials to which they are not entitled. This routine is not intended to provide a "login to the network" function, as such a function would involve the creation of new credentials rather than merely acquiring a handle to existing credentials. Such functions, if required, should be defined in implementation-specific extensions to the API.

If desired_name is GSS_C_NO_NAME, the call is interpreted as a request for a credential handle that will invoke default behavior when passed to gss_init_sec_context() (if cred_usage is GSS_C_INITIATE or GSS_C_BOTH) or gss_accept_sec_context() (if cred_usage is GSS_C_ACCEPT or GSS_C_BOTH).

Mechanisms should honor the desired_mechs parameter, and return a credential that is suitable to use only with the requested mechanisms. An exception to this is the case where one underlying credential element can be shared by multiple mechanisms;

in this case it is permissible for an implementation to indicate all mechanisms with which the credential element may be used. If desired_mechs is an empty set, behavior is undefined.

This routine is expected to be used primarily by context acceptors, since implementations are likely to provide mechanism-specific ways of obtaining GSS-API initiator credentials from the system login process. Some implementations may therefore not support the acquisition of GSS_C_INITIATE or GSS_C_BOTH credentials via gss_acquire_cred for any name other than GSS_C_NO_NAME, or a name produced by applying either gss_inquire_cred to a valid credential, or gss_inquire_context to an active context.

If credential acquisition is time-consuming for a mechanism, the mechanism may choose to delay the actual acquisition until the credential is required (e.g. by gss_init_sec_context or gss_accept_sec_context). Such mechanism-specific implementation decisions should be invisible to the calling application; thus a call of gss_inquire_cred immediately following the call of gss_acquire_cred must return valid credential data, and may therefore incur the overhead of a deferred credential acquisition.

Return value:

GSS_S_COMPLETE: Successful completion.

GSS_S_BAD_MECH: Unavailable mechanism requested.

GSS_S_BAD_NAMETYPE: Type contained within desired_name parameter is not supported.

GSS_S_BAD_NAME: Value supplied for desired_name parameter is ill formed.

GSS_S_CREDENTIALS_EXPIRED: The credentials could not be acquired Because they have expired.

GSS_S_NO_CRED: No credentials were found for the specified name.

gss_add_cred

OM_uint32 gss_add_cred (*OM_uint32* * `minor_status`, *const*   [Function]
     gss_cred_id_t `input_cred_handle`, *const gss_name_t* `desired_name`, *const*
     gss_OID `desired_mech`, *gss_cred_usage_t* `cred_usage`, *OM_uint32*
     `initiator_time_req`, *OM_uint32* `acceptor_time_req`, *gss_cred_id_t* *
     `output_cred_handle`, *gss_OID_set* * `actual_mechs`, *OM_uint32* *
     `initiator_time_rec`, *OM_uint32* * `acceptor_time_rec`)

minor_status: (integer, modify) Mechanism specific status code.

input_cred_handle: (gss_cred_id_t, read, optional) The credential to which a credential-element will be added. If GSS_C_NO_CREDENTIAL is specified, the routine will compose the new credential based on default behavior (see text). Note that, while the credential-handle is not modified by gss_add_cred(), the underlying credential will be modified if output_credential_handle is NULL.

desired_name: (gss_name_t, read.) Name of principal whose credential should be acquired.

desired_mech: (Object ID, read) Underlying security mechanism with which the credential may be used.

cred_usage: (gss_cred_usage_t, read) GSS_C_BOTH - Credential may be used either to initiate or accept security contexts. GSS_C_INITIATE - Credential will only be used to initiate security contexts. GSS_C_ACCEPT - Credential will only be used to accept security contexts.

initiator_time_req: (Integer, read, optional) number of seconds that the credential should remain valid for initiating security contexts. This argument is ignored if the composed credentials are of type GSS_C_ACCEPT. Specify GSS_C_INDEFINITE to request that the credentials have the maximum permitted initiator lifetime.

acceptor_time_req: (Integer, read, optional) number of seconds that the credential should remain valid for accepting security contexts. This argument is ignored if the composed credentials are of type GSS_C_INITIATE. Specify GSS_C_INDEFINITE to request that the credentials have the maximum permitted initiator lifetime.

output_cred_handle: (gss_cred_id_t, modify, optional) The returned credential handle, containing the new credential-element and all the credential-elements from input_cred_handle. If a valid pointer to a gss_cred_id_t is supplied for this parameter, gss_add_cred creates a new credential handle containing all credential-elements from the input_cred_handle and the newly acquired credential-element; if NULL is specified for this parameter, the newly acquired credential-element will be added to the credential identified by input_cred_handle. The resources associated with any credential handle returned via this parameter must be released by the application after use with a call to gss_release_cred().

actual_mechs: (Set of Object IDs, modify, optional) The complete set of mechanisms for which the new credential is valid. Storage for the returned OID-set must be freed by the application after use with a call to gss_release_oid_set(). Specify NULL if not required.

initiator_time_rec: (Integer, modify, optional) Actual number of seconds for which the returned credentials will remain valid for initiating contexts using the specified mechanism. If the implementation or mechanism does not support expiration of credentials, the value GSS_C_INDEFINITE will be returned. Specify NULL if not required

acceptor_time_rec: (Integer, modify, optional) Actual number of seconds for which the returned credentials will remain valid for accepting security contexts using the specified mechanism. If the implementation or mechanism does not support expiration of credentials, the value GSS_C_INDEFINITE will be returned. Specify NULL if not required

Adds a credential-element to a credential. The credential-element is identified by the name of the principal to which it refers. GSS-API implementations must impose a local access-control policy on callers of this routine to prevent unauthorized callers from acquiring credential-elements to which they are not entitled. This routine is not intended to provide a "login to the network" function, as such a function would involve the creation of new mechanism-specific authentication data, rather than merely acquiring a GSS-API handle to existing data. Such functions, if required, should be defined in implementation-specific extensions to the API.

If desired_name is GSS_C_NO_NAME, the call is interpreted as a request to add a credential element that will invoke default behavior when passed to gss_init_sec_context()

(if cred_usage is GSS_C_INITIATE or GSS_C_BOTH) or gss_accept_sec_context() (if cred_usage is GSS_C_ACCEPT or GSS_C_BOTH).

This routine is expected to be used primarily by context acceptors, since implementations are likely to provide mechanism-specific ways of obtaining GSS-API initiator credentials from the system login process. Some implementations may therefore not support the acquisition of GSS_C_INITIATE or GSS_C_BOTH credentials via gss_acquire_cred for any name other than GSS_C_NO_NAME, or a name produced by applying either gss_inquire_cred to a valid credential, or gss_inquire_context to an active context.

If credential acquisition is time-consuming for a mechanism, the mechanism may choose to delay the actual acquisition until the credential is required (e.g. by gss_init_sec_context or gss_accept_sec_context). Such mechanism-specific implementation decisions should be invisible to the calling application; thus a call of gss_inquire_cred immediately following the call of gss_add_cred must return valid credential data, and may therefore incur the overhead of a deferred credential acquisition.

This routine can be used to either compose a new credential containing all credential-elements of the original in addition to the newly-acquire credential-element, or to add the new credential- element to an existing credential. If NULL is specified for the output_cred_handle parameter argument, the new credential-element will be added to the credential identified by input_cred_handle; if a valid pointer is specified for the output_cred_handle parameter, a new credential handle will be created.

If GSS_C_NO_CREDENTIAL is specified as the input_cred_handle, gss_add_cred will compose a credential (and set the output_cred_handle parameter accordingly) based on default behavior. That is, the call will have the same effect as if the application had first made a call to gss_acquire_cred(), specifying the same usage and passing GSS_C_NO_NAME as the desired_name parameter to obtain an explicit credential handle embodying default behavior, passed this credential handle to gss_add_cred(), and finally called gss_release_cred() on the first credential handle.

If GSS_C_NO_CREDENTIAL is specified as the input_cred_handle parameter, a non-NULL output_cred_handle must be supplied.

Return value:

GSS_S_COMPLETE: Successful completion.

GSS_S_BAD_MECH: Unavailable mechanism requested.

GSS_S_BAD_NAMETYPE: Type contained within desired_name parameter is not supported.

GSS_S_BAD_NAME: Value supplied for desired_name parameter is ill-formed.

GSS_S_DUPLICATE_ELEMENT: The credential already contains an element for the requested mechanism with overlapping usage and validity period.

GSS_S_CREDENTIALS_EXPIRED: The required credentials could not be added because they have expired.

GSS_S_NO_CRED: No credentials were found for the specified name.

gss_inquire_cred

OM_uint32 gss_inquire_cred (*OM_uint32* * minor_status, *const*   [Function]
    gss_cred_id_t cred_handle, *gss_name_t* * name, *OM_uint32* * lifetime,
    gss_cred_usage_t * cred_usage, *gss_OID_set* * mechanisms)

minor_status: (integer, modify) Mechanism specific status code.

cred_handle: (gss_cred_id_t, read) A handle that refers to the target credential. Specify GSS_C_NO_CREDENTIAL to inquire about the default initiator principal.

name: (gss_name_t, modify, optional) The name whose identity the credential asserts. Storage associated with this name should be freed by the application after use with a call to gss_release_name(). Specify NULL if not required.

lifetime: (Integer, modify, optional) The number of seconds for which the credential will remain valid. If the credential has expired, this parameter will be set to zero. If the implementation does not support credential expiration, the value GSS_C_INDEFINITE will be returned. Specify NULL if not required.

cred_usage: (gss_cred_usage_t, modify, optional) How the credential may be used. One of the following: GSS_C_INITIATE, GSS_C_ACCEPT, GSS_C_BOTH. Specify NULL if not required.

mechanisms: (gss_OID_set, modify, optional) Set of mechanisms supported by the credential. Storage associated with this OID set must be freed by the application after use with a call to gss_release_oid_set(). Specify NULL if not required.

Obtains information about a credential.

Return value:

GSS_S_COMPLETE: Successful completion.

GSS_S_NO_CRED: The referenced credentials could not be accessed.

GSS_S_DEFECTIVE_CREDENTIAL: The referenced credentials were invalid.

GSS_S_CREDENTIALS_EXPIRED: The referenced credentials have expired. If the lifetime parameter was not passed as NULL, it will be set to 0.

gss_inquire_cred_by_mech

OM_uint32 gss_inquire_cred_by_mech (*OM_uint32* *   [Function]
    minor_status, *const gss_cred_id_t* cred_handle, *const gss_OID* mech_type,
    gss_name_t * name, *OM_uint32* * initiator_lifetime, *OM_uint32* *
    acceptor_lifetime, *gss_cred_usage_t* * cred_usage)

minor_status: (Integer, modify) Mechanism specific status code.

cred_handle: (gss_cred_id_t, read) A handle that refers to the target credential. Specify GSS_C_NO_CREDENTIAL to inquire about the default initiator principal.

mech_type: (gss_OID, read) The mechanism for which information should be returned.

name: (gss_name_t, modify, optional) The name whose identity the credential asserts. Storage associated with this name must be freed by the application after use with a call to gss_release_name(). Specify NULL if not required.

initiator_lifetime: (Integer, modify, optional) The number of seconds for which the credential will remain capable of initiating security contexts under the specified mechanism. If the credential can no longer be used to initiate contexts, or if the credential usage for this mechanism is GSS_C_ACCEPT, this parameter will be set to zero. If the implementation does not support expiration of initiator credentials, the value GSS_C_INDEFINITE will be returned. Specify NULL if not required.

acceptor_lifetime: (Integer, modify, optional) The number of seconds for which the credential will remain capable of accepting security contexts under the specified mechanism. If the credential can no longer be used to accept contexts, or if the credential usage for this mechanism is GSS_C_INITIATE, this parameter will be set to zero. If the implementation does not support expiration of acceptor credentials, the value GSS_C_INDEFINITE will be returned. Specify NULL if not required.

cred_usage: (gss_cred_usage_t, modify, optional) How the credential may be used with the specified mechanism. One of the following: GSS_C_INITIATE, GSS_C_ACCEPT, GSS_C_BOTH. Specify NULL if not required.

Obtains per-mechanism information about a credential.

Return value:

`GSS_S_COMPLETE`: Successful completion.

`GSS_S_NO_CRED`: The referenced credentials could not be accessed.

`GSS_S_DEFECTIVE_CREDENTIAL`: The referenced credentials were invalid.

`GSS_S_CREDENTIALS_EXPIRED`: The referenced credentials have expired. If the lifetime parameter was not passed as NULL, it will be set to 0.

gss_release_cred

OM_uint32 gss_release_cred (*OM_uint32 * minor_status*,   [Function]
       gss_cred_id_t * cred_handle)

minor_status: (Integer, modify) Mechanism specific status code.

cred_handle: (gss_cred_id_t, modify, optional) Opaque handle identifying credential to be released. If GSS_C_NO_CREDENTIAL is supplied, the routine will complete successfully, but will do nothing.

Informs GSS-API that the specified credential handle is no longer required by the application, and frees associated resources. The cred_handle is set to GSS_C_NO_CREDENTIAL on successful completion of this call.

Return value:

`GSS_S_COMPLETE`: Successful completion.

`GSS_S_NO_CRED`: Credentials could not be accessed.

3.6 Context-Level Routines

```
GSS-API Context-Level Routines


Routine                            Function
-------                            --------

gss_init_sec_context               Initiate a security context with
```

	a peer application.
gss_accept_sec_context	Accept a security context initiated by a peer application.
gss_delete_sec_context	Discard a security context.
gss_process_context_token	Process a token on a security context from a peer application.
gss_context_time	Determine for how long a context will remain valid.
gss_inquire_context	Obtain information about a security context.
gss_wrap_size_limit	Determine token-size limit for gss_wrap on a context.
gss_export_sec_context	Transfer a security context to another process.
gss_import_sec_context	Import a transferred context.

gss_init_sec_context

OM_uint32 gss_init_sec_context (*OM_uint32* * minor_status,   [Function]
        const gss_cred_id_t initiator_cred_handle, *gss_ctx_id_t* *
        context_handle, *const gss_name_t* target_name, *const gss_OID*
        mech_type, *OM_uint32* req_flags, *OM_uint32* time_req, *const*
        gss_channel_bindings_t input_chan_bindings, *const gss_buffer_t*
        input_token, *gss_OID* * actual_mech_type, *gss_buffer_t* output_token,
        OM_uint32 * ret_flags, *OM_uint32* * time_rec)

minor_status: (integer, modify) Mechanism specific status code.

initiator_cred_handle: (gss_cred_id_t, read, optional) Handle for credentials claimed. Supply GSS_C_NO_CREDENTIAL to act as a default initiator principal. If no default initiator is defined, the function will return GSS_S_NO_CRED.

context_handle: (gss_ctx_id_t, read/modify) Context handle for new context. Supply GSS_C_NO_CONTEXT for first call; use value returned by first call in continuation calls. Resources associated with this context-handle must be released by the application after use with a call to gss_delete_sec_context().

target_name: (gss_name_t, read) Name of target.

mech_type: (OID, read, optional) Object ID of desired mechanism. Supply GSS_C_NO_OID to obtain an implementation specific default.

req_flags: (bit-mask, read) Contains various independent flags, each of which requests that the context support a specific service option. Symbolic names are provided for each flag, and the symbolic names corresponding to the required flags should be logically-ORed together to form the bit-mask value. See below for the flags.

time_req: (Integer, read, optional) Desired number of seconds for which context should remain valid. Supply 0 to request a default validity period.

input_chan_bindings: (channel bindings, read, optional) Application-specified bindings. Allows application to securely bind channel identification information to the security context. Specify GSS_C_NO_CHANNEL_BINDINGS if channel bindings are not used.

input_token: (buffer, opaque, read, optional) Token received from peer application. Supply GSS_C_NO_BUFFER, or a pointer to a buffer containing the value GSS_C_EMPTY_BUFFER on initial call.

actual_mech_type: (OID, modify, optional) Actual mechanism used. The OID returned via this parameter will be a pointer to static storage that should be treated as read-only; In particular the application should not attempt to free it. Specify NULL if not required.

output_token: (buffer, opaque, modify) Token to be sent to peer application. If the length field of the returned buffer is zero, no token need be sent to the peer application. Storage associated with this buffer must be freed by the application after use with a call to gss_release_buffer().

ret_flags: (bit-mask, modify, optional) Contains various independent flags, each of which indicates that the context supports a specific service option. Specify NULL if not required. Symbolic names are provided for each flag, and the symbolic names corresponding to the required flags should be logically-ANDed with the ret_flags value to test whether a given option is supported by the context. See below for the flags.

time_rec: (Integer, modify, optional) Number of seconds for which the context will remain valid. If the implementation does not support context expiration, the value GSS_C_INDEFINITE will be returned. Specify NULL if not required.

Initiates the establishment of a security context between the application and a remote peer. Initially, the input_token parameter should be specified either as GSS_C_NO_BUFFER, or as a pointer to a gss_buffer_desc object whose length field contains the value zero. The routine may return a output_token which should be transferred to the peer application, where the peer application will present it to gss_accept_sec_context. If no token need be sent, gss_init_sec_context will indicate this by setting the length field of the output_token argument to zero. To complete the context establishment, one or more reply tokens may be required from the peer application; if so, gss_init_sec_context will return a status containing the supplementary information bit GSS_S_CONTINUE_NEEDED. In this case, gss_init_sec_context should be called again when the reply token is received from the peer application, passing the reply token to gss_init_sec_context via the input_token parameters.

Portable applications should be constructed to use the token length and return status to determine whether a token needs to be sent or waited for. Thus a typical portable caller should always invoke gss_init_sec_context within a loop:

```
int context_established = 0;
gss_ctx_id_t context_hdl = GSS_C_NO_CONTEXT;
        ...
input_token->length = 0;

while (!context_established) {
  maj_stat = gss_init_sec_context(&min_stat,
                                  cred_hdl,
                                  &context_hdl,
                                  target_name,
```

```
                                        desired_mech,
                                        desired_services,
                                        desired_time,
                                        input_bindings,
                                        input_token,
                                        &actual_mech,
                                        output_token,
                                        &actual_services,
                                        &actual_time);
    if (GSS_ERROR(maj_stat)) {
      report_error(maj_stat, min_stat);
    };

    if (output_token->length != 0) {
      send_token_to_peer(output_token);
      gss_release_buffer(&min_stat, output_token)
    };
    if (GSS_ERROR(maj_stat)) {

      if (context_hdl != GSS_C_NO_CONTEXT)
        gss_delete_sec_context(&min_stat,
                               &context_hdl,
                               GSS_C_NO_BUFFER);
      break;
    };

    if (maj_stat & GSS_S_CONTINUE_NEEDED) {
      receive_token_from_peer(input_token);
    } else {
      context_established = 1;
    };
  };
```

Whenever the routine returns a major status that includes the value GSS_S_CONTINUE_NEEDED, the context is not fully established and the following restrictions apply to the output parameters:

- The value returned via the time_rec parameter is undefined unless the accompanying ret_flags parameter contains the bit GSS_C_PROT_READY_FLAG, indicating that per-message services may be applied in advance of a successful completion status, the value returned via the actual_mech_type parameter is undefined until the routine returns a major status value of GSS_S_COMPLETE.

- The values of the GSS_C_DELEG_FLAG, GSS_C_MUTUAL_FLAG, GSS_C_REPLAY_FLAG, GSS_C_SEQUENCE_FLAG, GSS_C_CONF_FLAG, GSS_C_INTEG_FLAG and GSS_C_ANON_FLAG bits returned via the ret_flags parameter should contain the values that the implementation expects would be valid if context establishment were to succeed. In particular, if the application has requested a service such as delegation or anonymous authentication via the req_flags argument, and such a service is unavailable from the underlying mechanism, gss_init_sec_context should generate a token that will not provide the service, and indicate via the ret_flags argument that the service will not be supported. The application may choose to abort the context establishment by calling gss_delete_sec_context (if it cannot continue in the absence of the service), or it may choose to transmit the token and continue context establishment (if the service was merely desired but not mandatory).

- The values of the GSS_C_PROT_READY_FLAG and GSS_C_TRANS_FLAG bits within ret_flags should indicate the actual state at the time gss_init_sec_context returns, whether or not the context is fully established.

- GSS-API implementations that support per-message protection are encouraged to set the GSS_C_PROT_READY_FLAG in the final ret_flags returned to a caller (i.e. when accompanied by a GSS_S_COMPLETE status code). However, applications should not rely on this behavior as the flag was not defined in Version 1 of the GSS-API. Instead, applications should determine what per-message services are available after a successful context establishment according to the GSS_C_INTEG_FLAG and GSS_C_CONF_FLAG values.

- All other bits within the ret_flags argument should be set to zero.

If the initial call of gss_init_sec_context() fails, the implementation should not create a context object, and should leave the value of the context_handle parameter set to GSS_C_NO_CONTEXT to indicate this. In the event of a failure on a subsequent call, the implementation is permitted to delete the "half-built" security context (in which case it should set the context_handle parameter to GSS_C_NO_CONTEXT), but the preferred behavior is to leave the security context untouched for the application to delete (using gss_delete_sec_context).

During context establishment, the informational status bits GSS_S_OLD_TOKEN and GSS_S_DUPLICATE_TOKEN indicate fatal errors, and GSS-API mechanisms should always return them in association with a routine error of GSS_S_FAILURE. This requirement for pairing did not exist in version 1 of the GSS-API specification, so applications that wish to run over version 1 implementations must special-case these codes.

The **req_flags** values:

> GSS_C_DELEG_FLAG
>
> - True - Delegate credentials to remote peer.
> - False - Don't delegate.
>
> GSS_C_MUTUAL_FLAG
>
> - True - Request that remote peer authenticate itself.
> - False - Authenticate self to remote peer only.
>
> GSS_C_REPLAY_FLAG
>
> - True - Enable replay detection for messages protected with gss_wrap or gss_get_mic.
> - False - Don't attempt to detect replayed messages.

GSS_C_SEQUENCE_FLAG

- True - Enable detection of out-of-sequence protected messages.
- False - Don't attempt to detect out-of-sequence messages.

GSS_C_CONF_FLAG

- True - Request that confidentiality service be made available (via gss_wrap).
- False - No per-message confidentiality service is required.

GSS_C_INTEG_FLAG

- True - Request that integrity service be made available (via gss_wrap or gss_get_mic).
- False - No per-message integrity service is required.

GSS_C_ANON_FLAG

- True - Do not reveal the initiator's identity to the acceptor.
- False - Authenticate normally.

The ret_flags values:

GSS_C_DELEG_FLAG

- True - Credentials were delegated to the remote peer.
- False - No credentials were delegated.

GSS_C_MUTUAL_FLAG

- True - The remote peer has authenticated itself.
- False - Remote peer has not authenticated itself.

GSS_C_REPLAY_FLAG

- True - replay of protected messages will be detected.
- False - replayed messages will not be detected.

GSS_C_SEQUENCE_FLAG

- True - out-of-sequence protected messages will be detected.
- False - out-of-sequence messages will not be detected.

GSS_C_CONF_FLAG

- True - Confidentiality service may be invoked by calling gss_wrap routine.
- False - No confidentiality service (via gss_wrap) available. gss_wrap will provide message encapsulation, data-origin authentication and integrity services only.

GSS_C_INTEG_FLAG

- True - Integrity service may be invoked by calling either gss_get_mic or gss_wrap routines.
- False - Per-message integrity service unavailable.

GSS_C_ANON_FLAG

- True - The initiator's identity has not been revealed, and will not be revealed if any emitted token is passed to the acceptor.
- False - The initiator's identity has been or will be authenticated normally.

GSS_C_PROT_READY_FLAG

- True - Protection services (as specified by the states of the GSS_C_CONF_FLAG and GSS_C_INTEG_FLAG) are available for use if the accompanying major status return value is either GSS_S_COMPLETE or GSS_S_CONTINUE_NEEDED.
- False - Protection services (as specified by the states of the GSS_C_CONF_FLAG and GSS_C_INTEG_FLAG) are available only if the accompanying major status return value is GSS_S_COMPLETE.

GSS_C_TRANS_FLAG

- True - The resultant security context may be transferred to other processes via a call to gss_export_sec_context().
- False - The security context is not transferable.

All other bits should be set to zero.

Return value:

GSS_S_COMPLETE: Successful completion.

GSS_S_CONTINUE_NEEDED: Indicates that a token from the peer application is required to complete the context, and that gss_init_sec_context must be called again with that token.

GSS_S_DEFECTIVE_TOKEN: Indicates that consistency checks performed on the input_token failed.

GSS_S_DEFECTIVE_CREDENTIAL: Indicates that consistency checks performed on the credential failed.

GSS_S_NO_CRED: The supplied credentials were not valid for context initiation, or the credential handle did not reference any credentials.

GSS_S_CREDENTIALS_EXPIRED: The referenced credentials have expired.

GSS_S_BAD_BINDINGS: The input_token contains different channel bindings to those specified via the input_chan_bindings parameter.

GSS_S_BAD_SIG: The input_token contains an invalid MIC, or a MIC that could not be verified.

GSS_S_OLD_TOKEN: The input_token was too old. This is a fatal error during context establishment.

GSS_S_DUPLICATE_TOKEN: The input_token is valid, but is a duplicate of a token already processed. This is a fatal error during context establishment.

GSS_S_NO_CONTEXT: Indicates that the supplied context handle did not refer to a valid context.

GSS_S_BAD_NAMETYPE: The provided target_name parameter contained an invalid or unsupported type of name.

GSS_S_BAD_NAME: The provided target_name parameter was ill-formed.

GSS_S_BAD_MECH: The specified mechanism is not supported by the provided credential, or is unrecognized by the implementation.

gss_accept_sec_context

OM_uint32 gss_accept_sec_context (*OM_uint32* * minor_status,   [Function]
  gss_ctx_id_t * context_handle, *const gss_cred_id_t*
  acceptor_cred_handle, *const gss_buffer_t* input_token_buffer, *const*
  gss_channel_bindings_t input_chan_bindings, *gss_name_t* * src_name,
  gss_OID * mech_type, *gss_buffer_t* output_token, *OM_uint32* * ret_flags,
  OM_uint32 * time_rec, *gss_cred_id_t* * delegated_cred_handle)

minor_status: (Integer, modify) Mechanism specific status code.

context_handle: (gss_ctx_id_t, read/modify) Context handle for new context. Supply GSS_C_NO_CONTEXT for first call; use value returned in subsequent calls. Once gss_accept_sec_context() has returned a value via this parameter, resources have been assigned to the corresponding context, and must be freed by the application after use with a call to gss_delete_sec_context().

acceptor_cred_handle: (gss_cred_id_t, read) Credential handle claimed by context acceptor. Specify GSS_C_NO_CREDENTIAL to accept the context as a default principal. If GSS_C_NO_CREDENTIAL is specified, but no default acceptor principal is defined, GSS_S_NO_CRED will be returned.

input_token_buffer: (buffer, opaque, read) Token obtained from remote application.

input_chan_bindings: (channel bindings, read, optional) Application- specified bindings. Allows application to securely bind channel identification information to the security context. If channel bindings are not used, specify GSS_C_NO_CHANNEL_BINDINGS.

src_name: (gss_name_t, modify, optional) Authenticated name of context initiator. After use, this name should be deallocated by passing it to gss_release_name(). If not required, specify NULL.

mech_type: (Object ID, modify, optional) Security mechanism used. The returned OID value will be a pointer into static storage, and should be treated as read-only by the caller (in particular, it does not need to be freed). If not required, specify NULL.

output_token: (buffer, opaque, modify) Token to be passed to peer application. If the length field of the returned token buffer is 0, then no token need be passed to the peer application. If a non- zero length field is returned, the associated storage must be freed after use by the application with a call to gss_release_buffer().

ret_flags: (bit-mask, modify, optional) Contains various independent flags, each of which indicates that the context supports a specific service option. If not needed, specify NULL. Symbolic names are provided for each flag, and the symbolic names corresponding to the required flags should be logically-ANDed with the ret_flags value to test whether a given option is supported by the context. See below for the flags.

time_rec: (Integer, modify, optional) Number of seconds for which the context will remain valid. Specify NULL if not required.

delegated_cred_handle: (gss_cred_id_t, modify, optional credential) Handle for credentials received from context initiator. Only valid if deleg_flag in ret_flags is true, in which case an explicit credential handle (i.e. not GSS_C_NO_CREDENTIAL) will be returned; if deleg_flag is false, gss_accept_sec_context() will set this parameter to GSS_C_NO_CREDENTIAL. If a credential handle is returned, the associated resources must be released by the application after use with a call to gss_release_cred(). Specify NULL if not required.

Allows a remotely initiated security context between the application and a remote peer to be established. The routine may return a output_token which should be transferred to the peer application, where the peer application will present it to gss_init_sec_context. If no token need be sent, gss_accept_sec_context will indicate this by setting the length field of the output_token argument to zero. To complete the context establishment, one or more reply tokens may be required from the peer application; if so, gss_accept_sec_context will return a status flag of GSS_S_CONTINUE_NEEDED, in which case it should be called again when the reply token is received from the peer application, passing the token to gss_accept_sec_context via the input_token parameters.

Portable applications should be constructed to use the token length and return status to determine whether a token needs to be sent or waited for. Thus a typical portable caller should always invoke gss_accept_sec_context within a loop:

```
gss_ctx_id_t context_hdl = GSS_C_NO_CONTEXT;

do {
  receive_token_from_peer(input_token);
  maj_stat = gss_accept_sec_context(&min_stat,
                                    &context_hdl,
                                    cred_hdl,
                                    input_token,
                                    input_bindings,
                                    &client_name,
                                    &mech_type,
                                    output_token,
                                    &ret_flags,
                                    &time_rec,
                                    &deleg_cred);
  if (GSS_ERROR(maj_stat)) {
    report_error(maj_stat, min_stat);
  };
  if (output_token->length != 0) {
    send_token_to_peer(output_token);

    gss_release_buffer(&min_stat, output_token);
  };
  if (GSS_ERROR(maj_stat)) {
    if (context_hdl != GSS_C_NO_CONTEXT)
      gss_delete_sec_context(&min_stat,
```

```
                                &context_hdl,
                                GSS_C_NO_BUFFER);
            break;
        };
    } while (maj_stat & GSS_S_CONTINUE_NEEDED);
```

Whenever the routine returns a major status that includes the value GSS_S_CONTINUE_NEEDED, the context is not fully established and the following restrictions apply to the output parameters:

The value returned via the time_rec parameter is undefined Unless the accompanying ret_flags parameter contains the bit GSS_C_PROT_READY_FLAG, indicating that per-message services may be applied in advance of a successful completion status, the value returned via the mech_type parameter may be undefined until the routine returns a major status value of GSS_S_COMPLETE.

The values of the GSS_C_DELEG_FLAG, GSS_C_MUTUAL_FLAG,GSS_C_REPLAY_FLAG, GSS_C_SEQUENCE_FLAG,   GSS_C_CONF_FLAG,GSS_C_INTEG_FLAG   and GSS_C_ANON_FLAG bits returned via the ret_flags parameter should contain the values that the implementation expects would be valid if context establishment were to succeed.

The values of the GSS_C_PROT_READY_FLAG and GSS_C_TRANS_FLAG bits within ret_flags should indicate the actual state at the time gss_accept_sec_context returns, whether or not the context is fully established.

Although this requires that GSS-API implementations set the GSS_C_PROT_READY_FLAG in the final ret_flags returned to a caller (i.e.   when accompanied by a GSS_S_COMPLETE status code), applications should not rely on this behavior as the flag was not defined in Version 1 of the GSS-API. Instead, applications should be prepared to use per-message services after a successful context establishment, according to the GSS_C_INTEG_FLAG and GSS_C_CONF_FLAG values.

All other bits within the ret_flags argument should be set to zero. While the routine returns GSS_S_CONTINUE_NEEDED, the values returned via the ret_flags argument indicate the services that the implementation expects to be available from the established context.

If the initial call of gss_accept_sec_context() fails, the implementation should not create a context object, and should leave the value of the context_handle parameter set to GSS_C_NO_CONTEXT to indicate this. In the event of a failure on a subsequent call, the implementation is permitted to delete the "half-built" security context (in which case it should set the context_handle parameter to GSS_C_NO_CONTEXT), but the preferred behavior is to leave the security context (and the context_handle parameter) untouched for the application to delete (using gss_delete_sec_context).

During context establishment, the informational status bits GSS_S_OLD_TOKEN and GSS_S_DUPLICATE_TOKEN indicate fatal errors, and GSS-API mechanisms should always return them in association with a routine error of GSS_S_FAILURE. This requirement for pairing did not exist in version 1 of the GSS-API specification, so applications that wish to run over version 1 implementations must special-case these codes.

The **ret_flags** values:

`GSS_C_DELEG_FLAG`

- True - Delegated credentials are available via the delegated_cred_handle parameter.
- False - No credentials were delegated.

`GSS_C_MUTUAL_FLAG`

- True - Remote peer asked for mutual authentication.
- False - Remote peer did not ask for mutual authentication.

`GSS_C_REPLAY_FLAG`

- True - replay of protected messages will be detected.
- False - replayed messages will not be detected.

`GSS_C_SEQUENCE_FLAG`

- True - out-of-sequence protected messages will be detected.
- False - out-of-sequence messages will not be detected.

`GSS_C_CONF_FLAG`

- True - Confidentiality service may be invoked by calling the gss_wrap routine.
- False - No confidentiality service (via gss_wrap) available. gss_wrap will provide message encapsulation, data-origin authentication and integrity services only.

`GSS_C_INTEG_FLAG`

- True - Integrity service may be invoked by calling either gss_get_mic or gss_wrap routines.
- False - Per-message integrity service unavailable.

`GSS_C_ANON_FLAG`

- True - The initiator does not wish to be authenticated; the src_name parameter (if requested) contains an anonymous internal name.
- False - The initiator has been authenticated normally.

`GSS_C_PROT_READY_FLAG`

- True - Protection services (as specified by the states of the GSS_C_CONF_FLAG and GSS_C_INTEG_FLAG) are available if the accompanying major status return value is either GSS_S_COMPLETE or GSS_S_CONTINUE_NEEDED.
- False - Protection services (as specified by the states of the GSS_C_CONF_FLAG and GSS_C_INTEG_FLAG) are available only if the accompanying major status return value is GSS_S_COMPLETE.

`GSS_C_TRANS_FLAG`

- True - The resultant security context may be transferred to other processes via a call to gss_export_sec_context().

- False - The security context is not transferable.

All other bits should be set to zero.

Return value:

GSS_S_CONTINUE_NEEDED: Indicates that a token from the peer application is required to complete the context, and that gss_accept_sec_context must be called again with that token.

GSS_S_DEFECTIVE_TOKEN: Indicates that consistency checks performed on the input_token failed.

GSS_S_DEFECTIVE_CREDENTIAL: Indicates that consistency checks performed on the credential failed.

GSS_S_NO_CRED: The supplied credentials were not valid for context acceptance, or the credential handle did not reference any credentials.

GSS_S_CREDENTIALS_EXPIRED: The referenced credentials have expired.

GSS_S_BAD_BINDINGS: The input_token contains different channel bindings to those specified via the input_chan_bindings parameter.

GSS_S_NO_CONTEXT: Indicates that the supplied context handle did not refer to a valid context.

GSS_S_BAD_SIG: The input_token contains an invalid MIC.

GSS_S_OLD_TOKEN: The input_token was too old. This is a fatal error during context establishment.

GSS_S_DUPLICATE_TOKEN: The input_token is valid, but is a duplicate of a token already processed. This is a fatal error during context establishment.

GSS_S_BAD_MECH: The received token specified a mechanism that is not supported by the implementation or the provided credential.

gss_delete_sec_context

OM_uint32 gss_delete_sec_context (*OM_uint32 * minor_status*,   [Function]
    *gss_ctx_id_t * context_handle*, *gss_buffer_t output_token*)

minor_status: (Integer, modify) Mechanism specific status code.

context_handle: (gss_ctx_id_t, modify) Context handle identifying context to delete. After deleting the context, the GSS-API will set this context handle to GSS_C_NO_CONTEXT.

output_token: (buffer, opaque, modify, optional) Token to be sent to remote application to instruct it to also delete the context. It is recommended that applications specify GSS_C_NO_BUFFER for this parameter, requesting local deletion only. If a buffer parameter is provided by the application, the mechanism may return a token in it; mechanisms that implement only local deletion should set the length field of this token to zero to indicate to the application that no token is to be sent to the peer.

Delete a security context. gss_delete_sec_context will delete the local data structures associated with the specified security context, and may generate an output_token, which when passed to the peer gss_process_context_token will instruct it to do likewise. If no token is required by the mechanism, the GSS-API should set the length field of the output_token (if provided) to zero. No further security services may be obtained using the context specified by context_handle.

In addition to deleting established security contexts, gss_delete_sec_context must also be able to delete "half-built" security contexts resulting from an incomplete sequence of gss_init_sec_context()/gss_accept_sec_context() calls.

The output_token parameter is retained for compatibility with version 1 of the GSS-API. It is recommended that both peer applications invoke gss_delete_sec_context passing the value GSS_C_NO_BUFFER for the output_token parameter, indicating that no token is required, and that gss_delete_sec_context should simply delete local context data structures. If the application does pass a valid buffer to gss_delete_sec_context, mechanisms are encouraged to return a zero-length token, indicating that no peer action is necessary, and that no token should be transferred by the application.

Return value:

GSS_S_COMPLETE: Successful completion.

GSS_S_NO_CONTEXT: No valid context was supplied.

gss_process_context_token

OM_uint32 gss_process_context_token (*OM_uint32 **   [Function]
  minor_status, *const gss_ctx_id_t* **context_handle**, *const gss_buffer_t*
  token_buffer)

minor_status: (Integer, modify) Implementation specific status code.

context_handle: (gss_ctx_id_t, read) Context handle of context on which token is to be processed

token_buffer: (buffer, opaque, read) Token to process.

Provides a way to pass an asynchronous token to the security service. Most context-level tokens are emitted and processed synchronously by gss_init_sec_context and gss_accept_sec_context, and the application is informed as to whether further tokens are expected by the GSS_C_CONTINUE_NEEDED major status bit. Occasionally, a mechanism may need to emit a context-level token at a point when the peer entity is not expecting a token. For example, the initiator's final call to gss_init_sec_context may emit a token and return a status of GSS_S_COMPLETE, but the acceptor's call to gss_accept_sec_context may fail. The acceptor's mechanism may wish to send a token containing an error indication to the initiator, but the initiator is not expecting a token at this point, believing that the context is fully established. Gss_process_context_token provides a way to pass such a token to the mechanism at any time.

Return value:

GSS_S_COMPLETE: Successful completion.

GSS_S_DEFECTIVE_TOKEN: Indicates that consistency checks performed on the token failed.

GSS_S_NO_CONTEXT: The context_handle did not refer to a valid context.

gss_context_time

OM_uint32 **gss_context_time** (*OM_uint32 * **minor_status***, *const*   [Function]
     gss_ctx_id_t **context_handle**, *OM_uint32 * **time_rec***)

minor_status: (Integer, modify) Implementation specific status code.

context_handle: (gss_ctx_id_t, read) Identifies the context to be interrogated.

time_rec: (Integer, modify) Number of seconds that the context will remain valid. If the context has already expired, zero will be returned.

Determines the number of seconds for which the specified context will remain valid.

Return value:

GSS_S_COMPLETE: Successful completion.

GSS_S_CONTEXT_EXPIRED: The context has already expired.

GSS_S_NO_CONTEXT: The context_handle parameter did not identify a valid context

gss_inquire_context

OM_uint32 **gss_inquire_context** (*OM_uint32 * **minor_status***, *const*   [Function]
     gss_ctx_id_t **context_handle**, *gss_name_t * **src_name***, *gss_name_t **
     targ_name, *OM_uint32 * **lifetime_rec***, *gss_OID * **mech_type***, *OM_uint32*
     ** **ctx_flags***, *int * **locally_initiated***, *int * **open***)

minor_status: (Integer, modify) Mechanism specific status code.

context_handle: (gss_ctx_id_t, read) A handle that refers to the security context.

src_name: (gss_name_t, modify, optional) The name of the context initiator. If the context was established using anonymous authentication, and if the application invoking gss_inquire_context is the context acceptor, an anonymous name will be returned. Storage associated with this name must be freed by the application after use with a call to gss_release_name(). Specify NULL if not required.

targ_name: (gss_name_t, modify, optional) The name of the context acceptor. Storage associated with this name must be freed by the application after use with a call to gss_release_name(). If the context acceptor did not authenticate itself, and if the initiator did not specify a target name in its call to gss_init_sec_context(), the value GSS_C_NO_NAME will be returned. Specify NULL if not required.

lifetime_rec: (Integer, modify, optional) The number of seconds for which the context will remain valid. If the context has expired, this parameter will be set to zero. If the implementation does not support context expiration, the value GSS_C_INDEFINITE will be returned. Specify NULL if not required.

mech_type: (gss_OID, modify, optional) The security mechanism providing the context. The returned OID will be a pointer to static storage that should be treated as read-only by the application; in particular the application should not attempt to free it. Specify NULL if not required.

ctx_flags: (bit-mask, modify, optional) Contains various independent flags, each of which indicates that the context supports (or is expected to support, if ctx_open is false) a specific service option. If not needed, specify NULL. Symbolic names are provided for each flag, and the symbolic names corresponding to the required flags should be logically-ANDed with the ret_flags value to test whether a given option is supported by the context. See below for the flags.

locally_initiated: (Boolean, modify) Non-zero if the invoking application is the context initiator. Specify NULL if not required.

open: (Boolean, modify) Non-zero if the context is fully established; Zero if a context-establishment token is expected from the peer application. Specify NULL if not required.

Obtains information about a security context. The caller must already have obtained a handle that refers to the context, although the context need not be fully established.

The `ctx_flags` values:

GSS_C_DELEG_FLAG

- True - Credentials were delegated from the initiator to the acceptor.
- False - No credentials were delegated.

GSS_C_MUTUAL_FLAG

- True - The acceptor was authenticated to the initiator.
- False - The acceptor did not authenticate itself.

GSS_C_REPLAY_FLAG

- True - replay of protected messages will be detected.
- False - replayed messages will not be detected.

GSS_C_SEQUENCE_FLAG

- True - out-of-sequence protected messages will be detected.
- False - out-of-sequence messages will not be detected.

GSS_C_CONF_FLAG

- True - Confidentiality service may be invoked by calling gss_wrap routine.
- False - No confidentiality service (via gss_wrap) available. gss_wrap will provide message encapsulation, data-origin authentication and integrity services only.

GSS_C_INTEG_FLAG

- True - Integrity service may be invoked by calling either gss_get_mic or gss_wrap routines.
- False - Per-message integrity service unavailable.

GSS_C_ANON_FLAG

- True - The initiator's identity will not be revealed to the acceptor. The src_name parameter (if requested) contains an anonymous internal name.
- False - The initiator has been authenticated normally.

GSS_C_PROT_READY_FLAG

- True - Protection services (as specified by the states of the GSS_C_CONF_FLAG and GSS_C_INTEG_FLAG) are available for use.
- False - Protection services (as specified by the states of the GSS_C_CONF_FLAG and GSS_C_INTEG_FLAG) are available only if the context is fully established (i.e. if the open parameter is non-zero).

GSS_C_TRANS_FLAG

- True - The resultant security context may be transferred to other processes via a call to gss_export_sec_context().
- False - The security context is not transferable.

Return value:

GSS_S_COMPLETE: Successful completion.

GSS_S_NO_CONTEXT: The referenced context could not be accessed.

gss_wrap_size_limit

OM_uint32 gss_wrap_size_limit (*OM_uint32 * minor_status*, *const*   [Function]
     gss_ctx_id_t context_handle, *int* conf_req_flag, *gss_qop_t* qop_req,
     OM_uint32 req_output_size, *OM_uint32 * max_input_size*)

minor_status: (Integer, modify) Mechanism specific status code.

context_handle: (gss_ctx_id_t, read) A handle that refers to the security over which the messages will be sent.

conf_req_flag: (Boolean, read) Indicates whether gss_wrap will be asked to apply confidentiality protection in addition to integrity protection. See the routine description for gss_wrap for more details.

qop_req: (gss_qop_t, read) Indicates the level of protection that gss_wrap will be asked to provide. See the routine description for gss_wrap for more details.

req_output_size: (Integer, read) The desired maximum size for tokens emitted by gss_wrap.

max_input_size: (Integer, modify) The maximum input message size that may be presented to gss_wrap in order to guarantee that the emitted token shall be no larger than req_output_size bytes.

Allows an application to determine the maximum message size that, if presented to gss_wrap with the same conf_req_flag and qop_req parameters, will result in an output token containing no more than req_output_size bytes.

This call is intended for use by applications that communicate over protocols that impose a maximum message size. It enables the application to fragment messages prior to applying protection.

GSS-API implementations are recommended but not required to detect invalid QOP values when gss_wrap_size_limit() is called. This routine guarantees only a maximum message size, not the availability of specific QOP values for message protection.

Successful completion of this call does not guarantee that gss_wrap will be able to protect a message of length max_input_size bytes, since this ability may depend on the availability of system resources at the time that gss_wrap is called. However, if the implementation itself imposes an upper limit on the length of messages that may be processed by gss_wrap, the implementation should not return a value via max_input_bytes that is greater than this length.

Return value:

GSS_S_COMPLETE: Successful completion.

GSS_S_NO_CONTEXT: The referenced context could not be accessed.

GSS_S_CONTEXT_EXPIRED: The context has expired.

GSS_S_BAD_QOP: The specified QOP is not supported by the mechanism.

gss_export_sec_context

OM_uint32 gss_export_sec_context (*OM_uint32 * minor_status*,   [Function]
      *gss_ctx_id_t * context_handle*, *gss_buffer_t interprocess_token*)

minor_status: (Integer, modify) Mechanism specific status code.

context_handle: (gss_ctx_id_t, modify) Context handle identifying the context to transfer.

interprocess_token: (buffer, opaque, modify) Token to be transferred to target process. Storage associated with this token must be freed by the application after use with a call to gss_release_buffer().

Provided to support the sharing of work between multiple processes. This routine will typically be used by the context-acceptor, in an application where a single process receives incoming connection requests and accepts security contexts over them, then passes the established context to one or more other processes for message exchange. gss_export_sec_context() deactivates the security context for the calling process and creates an interprocess token which, when passed to gss_import_sec_context in another process, will re-activate the context in the second process. Only a single instantiation of a given context may be active at any one time; a subsequent attempt by a context exporter to access the exported security context will fail.

The implementation may constrain the set of processes by which the interprocess token may be imported, either as a function of local security policy, or as a result of implementation decisions. For example, some implementations may constrain contexts to be passed only between processes that run under the same account, or which are part of the same process group.

The interprocess token may contain security-sensitive information (for example cryptographic keys). While mechanisms are encouraged to either avoid placing such sensitive information within interprocess tokens, or to encrypt the token before returning it to the application, in a typical object-library GSS-API implementation this may not be possible. Thus the application must take care to protect the interprocess token, and ensure that any process to which the token is transferred is trustworthy.

If creation of the interprocess token is successful, the implementation shall deallocate all process-wide resources associated with the security context, and set the context_handle to GSS_C_NO_CONTEXT. In the event of an error that makes it impossible to complete the export of the security context, the implementation must not return an interprocess token, and should strive to leave the security context referenced by the context-handle parameter untouched. If this is impossible, it is permissible for the implementation to delete the security context, providing it also sets the context-handle parameter to GSS_C_NO_CONTEXT.

Return value:

GSS_S_COMPLETE: Successful completion.

GSS_S_CONTEXT_EXPIRED: The context has expired.

GSS_S_NO_CONTEXT: The context was invalid.

GSS_S_UNAVAILABLE: The operation is not supported.

gss_import_sec_context

OM_uint32 gss_import_sec_context (*OM_uint32 * minor_status*,   [Function]
     const gss_buffer_t **interprocess_token**, *gss_ctx_id_t * **context_handle**)
minor_status: (Integer, modify) Mechanism specific status code.

interprocess_token: (buffer, opaque, modify) Token received from exporting process

context_handle: (gss_ctx_id_t, modify) Context handle of newly reactivated context. Resources associated with this context handle must be released by the application after use with a call to gss_delete_sec_context().

Allows a process to import a security context established by another process. A given interprocess token may be imported only once. See gss_export_sec_context.

Return value:

GSS_S_COMPLETE: Successful completion.

GSS_S_NO_CONTEXT: The token did not contain a valid context reference.

GSS_S_DEFECTIVE_TOKEN: The token was invalid.

GSS_S_UNAVAILABLE: The operation is unavailable.

GSS_S_UNAUTHORIZED: Local policy prevents the import of this context by the current process.

3.7 Per-Message Routines

GSS-API Per-message Routines

Routine	Function
gss_get_mic	Calculate a cryptographic message integrity code (MIC) for a message; integrity service.
gss_verify_mic	Check a MIC against a message; verify integrity of a received message.
gss_wrap	Attach a MIC to a message, and optionally encrypt the message content. confidentiality service
gss_unwrap	Verify a message with attached

```
                                        MIC, and decrypt message content
                                        if necessary.
```

gss_get_mic

OM_uint32 gss_get_mic (*OM_uint32* * minor_status, *const*   [Function]
        gss_ctx_id_t context_handle, *gss_qop_t* qop_req, *const gss_buffer_t*
        message_buffer, *gss_buffer_t* message_token)

minor_status: (Integer, modify) Mechanism specific status code.

context_handle: (gss_ctx_id_t, read) Identifies the context on which the message will be sent.

qop_req: (gss_qop_t, read, optional) Specifies requested quality of protection. Callers are encouraged, on portability grounds, to accept the default quality of protection offered by the chosen mechanism, which may be requested by specifying GSS_C_QOP_DEFAULT for this parameter. If an unsupported protection strength is requested, gss_get_mic will return a major_status of GSS_S_BAD_QOP.

message_buffer: (buffer, opaque, read) Message to be protected.

message_token: (buffer, opaque, modify) Buffer to receive token. The application must free storage associated with this buffer after use with a call to gss_release_buffer().

Generates a cryptographic MIC for the supplied message, and places the MIC in a token for transfer to the peer application. The qop_req parameter allows a choice between several cryptographic algorithms, if supported by the chosen mechanism.

Since some application-level protocols may wish to use tokens emitted by gss_wrap() to provide "secure framing", implementations must support derivation of MICs from zero-length messages.

Return value:

GSS_S_COMPLETE: Successful completion.

GSS_S_CONTEXT_EXPIRED: The context has already expired.

GSS_S_NO_CONTEXT: The context_handle parameter did not identify a valid context.

GSS_S_BAD_QOP: The specified QOP is not supported by the mechanism.

gss_verify_mic

OM_uint32 gss_verify_mic (*OM_uint32* * minor_status, *const*   [Function]
        gss_ctx_id_t context_handle, *const gss_buffer_t* message_buffer, *const*
        gss_buffer_t token_buffer, *gss_qop_t* * qop_state)

minor_status: (Integer, modify) Mechanism specific status code.

context_handle: (gss_ctx_id_t, read) Identifies the context on which the message arrived.

message_buffer: (buffer, opaque, read) Message to be verified.

token_buffer: (buffer, opaque, read) Token associated with message.

qop_state: (gss_qop_t, modify, optional) Quality of protection gained from MIC Specify NULL if not required.

Verifies that a cryptographic MIC, contained in the token parameter, fits the supplied message. The qop_state parameter allows a message recipient to determine the strength of protection that was applied to the message.

Since some application-level protocols may wish to use tokens emitted by gss_wrap() to provide "secure framing", implementations must support the calculation and verification of MICs over zero-length messages.

Return value:

`GSS_S_COMPLETE`: Successful completion.

`GSS_S_DEFECTIVE_TOKEN`: The token failed consistency checks.

`GSS_S_BAD_SIG`: The MIC was incorrect.

`GSS_S_DUPLICATE_TOKEN`: The token was valid, and contained a correct MIC for the message, but it had already been processed.

`GSS_S_OLD_TOKEN`: The token was valid, and contained a correct MIC for the message, but it is too old to check for duplication.

`GSS_S_UNSEQ_TOKEN`: The token was valid, and contained a correct MIC for the message, but has been verified out of sequence; a later token has already been received.

`GSS_S_GAP_TOKEN`: The token was valid, and contained a correct MIC for the message, but has been verified out of sequence; an earlier expected token has not yet been received.

`GSS_S_CONTEXT_EXPIRED`: The context has already expired.

`GSS_S_NO_CONTEXT`: The context_handle parameter did not identify a valid context.

gss_wrap

OM_uint32 gss_wrap (*OM_uint32* * `minor_status`, *const gss_ctx_id_t*   [Function]
        `context_handle`, *int* `conf_req_flag`, *gss_qop_t* `qop_req`, *const gss_buffer_t*
        `input_message_buffer`, *int* * `conf_state`, *gss_buffer_t*
        `output_message_buffer`)

minor_status: (Integer, modify) Mechanism specific status code.

context_handle: (gss_ctx_id_t, read) Identifies the context on which the message will be sent.

conf_req_flag: (boolean, read) Non-zero - Both confidentiality and integrity services are requested. Zero - Only integrity service is requested.

qop_req: (gss_qop_t, read, optional) Specifies required quality of protection. A mechanism-specific default may be requested by setting qop_req to GSS_C_QOP_DEFAULT. If an unsupported protection strength is requested, gss_wrap will return a major_status of GSS_S_BAD_QOP.

input_message_buffer: (buffer, opaque, read) Message to be protected.

conf_state: (boolean, modify, optional) Non-zero - Confidentiality, data origin authentication and integrity services have been applied. Zero - Integrity and data origin services only has been applied. Specify NULL if not required.

output_message_buffer: (buffer, opaque, modify) Buffer to receive protected message. Storage associated with this message must be freed by the application after use with a call to gss_release_buffer().

Attaches a cryptographic MIC and optionally encrypts the specified input_message. The output_message contains both the MIC and the message. The qop_req parameter allows a choice between several cryptographic algorithms, if supported by the chosen mechanism.

Since some application-level protocols may wish to use tokens emitted by gss_wrap() to provide "secure framing", implementations must support the wrapping of zero-length messages.

Return value:

GSS_S_COMPLETE: Successful completion.

GSS_S_CONTEXT_EXPIRED: The context has already expired.

GSS_S_NO_CONTEXT: The context_handle parameter did not identify a valid context.

GSS_S_BAD_QOP: The specified QOP is not supported by the mechanism.

gss_unwrap

OM_uint32 gss_unwrap (*OM_uint32 * minor_status*, const   [Function]
    gss_ctx_id_t context_handle, *const gss_buffer_t* input_message_buffer,
    gss_buffer_t output_message_buffer, *int * conf_state*, *gss_qop_t ***
    qop_state)

minor_status: (Integer, modify) Mechanism specific status code.

context_handle: (gss_ctx_id_t, read) Identifies the context on which the message arrived.

input_message_buffer: (buffer, opaque, read) Protected message.

output_message_buffer: (buffer, opaque, modify) Buffer to receive unwrapped message. Storage associated with this buffer must be freed by the application after use use with a call to gss_release_buffer().

conf_state: (boolean, modify, optional) Non-zero - Confidentiality and integrity protection were used. Zero - Integrity service only was used. Specify NULL if not required.

qop_state: (gss_qop_t, modify, optional) Quality of protection provided. Specify NULL if not required.

Converts a message previously protected by gss_wrap back to a usable form, verifying the embedded MIC. The conf_state parameter indicates whether the message was encrypted; the qop_state parameter indicates the strength of protection that was used to provide the confidentiality and integrity services.

Since some application-level protocols may wish to use tokens emitted by gss_wrap() to provide "secure framing", implementations must support the wrapping and un-wrapping of zero-length messages.

Return value:

GSS_S_COMPLETE: Successful completion.

GSS_S_DEFECTIVE_TOKEN: The token failed consistency checks.

GSS_S_BAD_SIG: The MIC was incorrect.

GSS_S_DUPLICATE_TOKEN: The token was valid, and contained a correct MIC for the message, but it had already been processed.

GSS_S_OLD_TOKEN: The token was valid, and contained a correct MIC for the message, but it is too old to check for duplication.

GSS_S_UNSEQ_TOKEN: The token was valid, and contained a correct MIC for the message, but has been verified out of sequence; a later token has already been received.

GSS_S_GAP_TOKEN: The token was valid, and contained a correct MIC for the message, but has been verified out of sequence; an earlier expected token has not yet been received.

GSS_S_CONTEXT_EXPIRED: The context has already expired.

GSS_S_NO_CONTEXT: The context_handle parameter did not identify a valid context.

3.8 Name Manipulation

GSS-API Name manipulation Routines

```
Routine                         Function
-------                         --------

gss_import_name                 Convert a contiguous string name
                                to internal-form.

gss_display_name                Convert internal-form name to
                                text.

gss_compare_name                Compare two internal-form names.
gss_release_name                Discard an internal-form name.
gss_inquire_names_for_mech      List the name-types supported by.
                                the specified mechanism.

gss_inquire_mechs_for_name      List mechanisms that support the
                                specified name-type.

gss_canonicalize_name           Convert an internal name to an MN.
gss_export_name                 Convert an MN to export form.
gss_duplicate_name              Create a copy of an internal name.
```

gss_import_name

OM_uint32 gss_import_name (*OM_uint32 * minor_status*, *const*   [Function]
  gss_buffer_t **input_name_buffer**, *const gss_OID* **input_name_type**,
  gss_name_t * **output_name**)

minor_status: (Integer, modify) Mechanism specific status code.

input_name_buffer: (buffer, octet-string, read) Buffer containing contiguous string name to convert.

input_name_type: (Object ID, read, optional) Object ID specifying type of printable name. Applications may specify either GSS_C_NO_OID to use a mechanism-specific default printable syntax, or an OID recognized by the GSS-API implementation to name a specific namespace.

output_name: (gss_name_t, modify) Returned name in internal form. Storage associated with this name must be freed by the application after use with a call to gss_release_name().

Convert a contiguous string name to internal form. In general, the internal name returned (via the @output_name parameter) will not be an MN; the exception to this is if the @input_name_type indicates that the contiguous string provided via the @input_name_buffer parameter is of type GSS_C_NT_EXPORT_NAME, in which case the returned internal name will be an MN for the mechanism that exported the name.

Return value:

GSS_S_COMPLETE: Successful completion.

GSS_S_BAD_NAMETYPE: The input_name_type was unrecognized.

GSS_S_BAD_NAME: The input_name parameter could not be interpreted as a name of the specified type.

GSS_S_BAD_MECH: The input name-type was GSS_C_NT_EXPORT_NAME, but the mechanism contained within the input-name is not supported.

gss_display_name

OM_uint32 gss_display_name (*OM_uint32* * minor_status, *const*   [Function]
    gss_name_t input_name, *gss_buffer_t* output_name_buffer, *gss_OID* *
    output_name_type)

minor_status: (Integer, modify) Mechanism specific status code.

input_name: (gss_name_t, read) Name to be displayed.

output_name_buffer: (buffer, character-string, modify) Buffer to receive textual name string. The application must free storage associated with this name after use with a call to gss_release_buffer().

output_name_type: (Object ID, modify, optional) The type of the returned name. The returned gss_OID will be a pointer into static storage, and should be treated as read-only by the caller (in particular, the application should not attempt to free it). Specify NULL if not required.

Allows an application to obtain a textual representation of an opaque internal-form name for display purposes. The syntax of a printable name is defined by the GSS-API implementation.

If input_name denotes an anonymous principal, the implementation should return the gss_OID value GSS_C_NT_ANONYMOUS as the output_name_type, and a textual name that is syntactically distinct from all valid supported printable names in output_name_buffer.

If input_name was created by a call to gss_import_name, specifying GSS_C_NO_OID as the name-type, implementations that employ lazy conversion between name types may return GSS_C_NO_OID via the output_name_type parameter.

Return value:

GSS_S_COMPLETE: Successful completion.

GSS_S_BAD_NAME: @input_name was ill-formed.

gss_compare_name

OM_uint32 gss_compare_name (*OM_uint32* * `minor_status`, *const*   [Function]
      gss_name_t `name1`, *const gss_name_t* `name2`, *int* * `name_equal`)

> *minor_status*: (Integer, modify) Mechanism specific status code.

> *name1*: (gss_name_t, read) Internal-form name.

> *name2*: (gss_name_t, read) Internal-form name.

> *name_equal*: (boolean, modify) Non-zero - names refer to same entity. Zero - names refer to different entities (strictly, the names are not known to refer to the same identity).

> Allows an application to compare two internal-form names to determine whether they refer to the same entity.

> If either name presented to gss_compare_name denotes an anonymous principal, the routines should indicate that the two names do not refer to the same identity.

> Return value:

> GSS_S_COMPLETE: Successful completion.

> GSS_S_BAD_NAMETYPE: The two names were of incomparable types.

> GSS_S_BAD_NAME: One or both of name1 or name2 was ill-formed.

gss_release_name

OM_uint32 gss_release_name (*OM_uint32* * `minor_status`,   [Function]
      gss_name_t * `name`)

> *minor_status*: (Integer, modify) Mechanism specific status code.

> *name*: (gss_name_t, modify) The name to be deleted.

> Free GSSAPI-allocated storage associated with an internal-form name. The name is set to GSS_C_NO_NAME on successful completion of this call.

> Return value:

> GSS_S_COMPLETE: Successful completion.

> GSS_S_BAD_NAME: The name parameter did not contain a valid name.

gss_inquire_names_for_mech

OM_uint32 gss_inquire_names_for_mech (*OM_uint32* *   [Function]
      `minor_status`, *const gss_OID* `mechanism`, *gss_OID_set* * `name_types`)

> *minor_status*: (Integer, modify) Mechanism specific status code.

> *mechanism*: (gss_OID, read) The mechanism to be interrogated.

> *name_types*: (gss_OID_set, modify) Set of name-types supported by the specified mechanism. The returned OID set must be freed by the application after use with a call to gss_release_oid_set().

> Returns the set of nametypes supported by the specified mechanism.

> Return value:

> GSS_S_COMPLETE: Successful completion.

gss_inquire_mechs_for_name

OM_uint32 gss_inquire_mechs_for_name (*OM_uint32 **   [Function]
      minor_status, *const gss_name_t* input_name, *gss_OID_set ** mech_types)

minor_status: (Integer, modify) Mechanism specific status code.

input_name: (gss_name_t, read) The name to which the inquiry relates.

mech_types: (gss_OID_set, modify) Set of mechanisms that may support the specified name. The returned OID set must be freed by the caller after use with a call to gss_release_oid_set().

Returns the set of mechanisms supported by the GSS-API implementation that may be able to process the specified name.

Each mechanism returned will recognize at least one element within the name. It is permissible for this routine to be implemented within a mechanism-independent GSS-API layer, using the type information contained within the presented name, and based on registration information provided by individual mechanism implementations. This means that the returned mech_types set may indicate that a particular mechanism will understand the name when in fact it would refuse to accept the name as input to gss_canonicalize_name, gss_init_sec_context, gss_acquire_cred or gss_add_cred (due to some property of the specific name, as opposed to the name type). Thus this routine should be used only as a prefilter for a call to a subsequent mechanism-specific routine.

Return value:

GSS_S_COMPLETE: Successful completion.

GSS_S_BAD_NAME: The input_name parameter was ill-formed.

GSS_S_BAD_NAMETYPE: The input_name parameter contained an invalid or unsupported type of name.

gss_canonicalize_name

OM_uint32 gss_canonicalize_name (*OM_uint32 ** minor_status,   [Function]
     const gss_name_t input_name, *const gss_OID* mech_type, *gss_name_t **
     output_name)

minor_status: (Integer, modify) Mechanism specific status code.

input_name: (gss_name_t, read) The name for which a canonical form is desired.

mech_type: (Object ID, read) The authentication mechanism for which the canonical form of the name is desired. The desired mechanism must be specified explicitly; no default is provided.

output_name: (gss_name_t, modify) The resultant canonical name. Storage associated with this name must be freed by the application after use with a call to gss_release_name().

Generate a canonical mechanism name (MN) from an arbitrary internal name. The mechanism name is the name that would be returned to a context acceptor on successful authentication of a context where the initiator used the input_name in a successful call to gss_acquire_cred, specifying an OID set containing @mech_type as its only member, followed by a call to gss_init_sec_context(), specifying @mech_type as the authentication mechanism.

Return value:

GSS_S_COMPLETE: Successful completion.

gss_export_name

OM_uint32 **gss_export_name** (*OM_uint32* * **minor_status**, *const*   [Function]
      gss_name_t **input_name**, *gss_buffer_t* **exported_name**)
    minor_status: (Integer, modify) Mechanism specific status code.

    input_name: (gss_name_t, read) The MN to be exported.

    exported_name: (gss_buffer_t, octet-string, modify) The canonical contiguous string form of @input_name. Storage associated with this string must freed by the application after use with gss_release_buffer().

    To produce a canonical contiguous string representation of a mechanism name (MN), suitable for direct comparison (e.g. with memcmp) for use in authorization functions (e.g. matching entries in an access-control list). The @input_name parameter must specify a valid MN (i.e. an internal name generated by gss_accept_sec_context() or by gss_canonicalize_name()).

    Return value:

    GSS_S_COMPLETE: Successful completion.

    GSS_S_NAME_NOT_MN: The provided internal name was not a mechanism name.

    GSS_S_BAD_NAME: The provided internal name was ill-formed.

    GSS_S_BAD_NAMETYPE: The internal name was of a type not supported by the GSS-API implementation.

gss_duplicate_name

OM_uint32 **gss_duplicate_name** (*OM_uint32* * **minor_status**, *const*   [Function]
      gss_name_t **src_name**, *gss_name_t* * **dest_name**)
    minor_status: (Integer, modify) Mechanism specific status code.

    src_name: (gss_name_t, read) Internal name to be duplicated.

    dest_name: (gss_name_t, modify) The resultant copy of @src_name. Storage associated with this name must be freed by the application after use with a call to gss_release_name().

    Create an exact duplicate of the existing internal name @src_name. The new @dest_name will be independent of src_name (i.e. @src_name and @dest_name must both be released, and the release of one shall not affect the validity of the other).

    Return value:

    GSS_S_COMPLETE: Successful completion.

    GSS_S_BAD_NAME: The src_name parameter was ill-formed.

3.9 Miscellaneous Routines

GSS-API Miscellaneous Routines

```
Routine                        Function
-------                        --------
gss_add_oid_set_member         Add an object identifier to
                               a set.
gss_display_status             Convert a GSS-API status code
                               to text.
gss_indicate_mechs             Determine available underlying
                               authentication mechanisms.
gss_release_buffer             Discard a buffer.
gss_release_oid_set            Discard a set of object
                               identifiers.
gss_create_empty_oid_set       Create a set containing no
                               object identifiers.
gss_test_oid_set_member        Determines whether an object
                               identifier is a member of a set.
gss_encapsulate_token          Encapsulate a context token.
gss_decapsulate_token          Decapsulate a context token.
gss_oid_equal                  Compare two OIDs for equality.
```

gss_add_oid_set_member

OM_uint32 gss_add_oid_set_member (*OM_uint32 * minor_status*,   [Function]
     const gss_OID member_oid, *gss_OID_set * oid_set*)
    minor_status: (integer, modify) Mechanism specific status code.

    member_oid: (Object ID, read) The object identifier to copied into the set.

    oid_set: (Set of Object ID, modify) The set in which the object identifier should be inserted.

    Add an Object Identifier to an Object Identifier set. This routine is intended for use in conjunction with gss_create_empty_oid_set when constructing a set of mechanism OIDs for input to gss_acquire_cred. The oid_set parameter must refer to an OID-set that was created by GSS-API (e.g. a set returned by gss_create_empty_oid_set()). GSS-API creates a copy of the member_oid and inserts this copy into the set, expanding the storage allocated to the OID-set's elements array if necessary. The routine may add the new member OID anywhere within the elements array, and implementations should verify that the new member_oid is not already contained within the elements array; if the member_oid is already present, the oid_set should remain unchanged.

    Return value:

    GSS_S_COMPLETE: Successful completion.

gss_display_status

OM_uint32 gss_display_status (*OM_uint32* * `minor_status`,   [Function]
        OM_uint32 `status_value`, *int* `status_type`, *const gss_OID* `mech_type`,
        OM_uint32 * `message_context`, *gss_buffer_t* `status_string`)

minor_status: (integer, modify) Mechanism specific status code.

status_value: (Integer, read) Status value to be converted.

status_type: (Integer, read) GSS_C_GSS_CODE - status_value is a GSS status code. GSS_C_MECH_CODE - status_value is a mechanism status code.

mech_type: (Object ID, read, optional) Underlying mechanism (used to interpret a minor status value). Supply GSS_C_NO_OID to obtain the system default.

message_context: (Integer, read/modify) Should be initialized to zero by the application prior to the first call. On return from gss_display_status(), a non-zero status_value parameter indicates that additional messages may be extracted from the status code via subsequent calls to gss_display_status(), passing the same status_value, status_type, mech_type, and message_context parameters.

status_string: (buffer, character string, modify) Textual interpretation of the status_value. Storage associated with this parameter must be freed by the application after use with a call to gss_release_buffer().

Allows an application to obtain a textual representation of a GSS-API status code, for display to the user or for logging purposes. Since some status values may indicate multiple conditions, applications may need to call gss_display_status multiple times, each call generating a single text string. The message_context parameter is used by gss_display_status to store state information about which error messages have already been extracted from a given status_value; message_context must be initialized to 0 by the application prior to the first call, and gss_display_status will return a non-zero value in this parameter if there are further messages to extract.

The message_context parameter contains all state information required by gss_display_status in order to extract further messages from the status_value; even when a non-zero value is returned in this parameter, the application is not required to call gss_display_status again unless subsequent messages are desired. The following code extracts all messages from a given status code and prints them to stderr:

```
OM_uint32 message_context;
OM_uint32 status_code;
OM_uint32 maj_status;
OM_uint32 min_status;
gss_buffer_desc status_string;

    ...

message_context = 0;

do {
  maj_status = gss_display_status (
```

```
                              &min_status,
                              status_code,
                              GSS_C_GSS_CODE,
                              GSS_C_NO_OID,
                              &message_context,
                              &status_string)

          fprintf(stderr,
                  "%.*s\n",
                  (int)status_string.length,

                  (char *)status_string.value);

          gss_release_buffer(&min_status, &status_string);

        } while (message_context != 0);
```

Return value:

`GSS_S_COMPLETE`: Successful completion.

`GSS_S_BAD_MECH`: Indicates that translation in accordance with an unsupported mechanism type was requested.

`GSS_S_BAD_STATUS`: The status value was not recognized, or the status type was neither GSS_C_GSS_CODE nor GSS_C_MECH_CODE.

gss_indicate_mechs

`OM_uint32 gss_indicate_mechs` (*OM_uint32 * minor_status*,   [Function]
        gss_OID_set * `mech_set`)

minor_status: (integer, modify) Mechanism specific status code.

mech_set: (set of Object IDs, modify) Set of implementation-supported mechanisms. The returned gss_OID_set value will be a dynamically-allocated OID set, that should be released by the caller after use with a call to gss_release_oid_set().

Allows an application to determine which underlying security mechanisms are available.

Return value:

`GSS_S_COMPLETE`: Successful completion.

gss_release_buffer

`OM_uint32 gss_release_buffer` (*OM_uint32 * minor_status*,   [Function]
        gss_buffer_t `buffer`)

minor_status: (integer, modify) Mechanism specific status code.

buffer: (buffer, modify) The storage associated with the buffer will be deleted. The gss_buffer_desc object will not be freed, but its length field will be zeroed.

Free storage associated with a buffer. The storage must have been allocated by a GSS-API routine. In addition to freeing the associated storage, the routine will zero the length field in the descriptor to which the buffer parameter refers, and implementations are encouraged to additionally set the pointer field in the descriptor to NULL. Any buffer object returned by a GSS-API routine may be passed to gss_release_buffer (even if there is no storage associated with the buffer).

Return value:

`GSS_S_COMPLETE`: Successful completion.

gss_release_oid_set

`OM_uint32 gss_release_oid_set` (*OM_uint32* * `minor_status`,   [Function]
          gss_OID_set * `set`)

minor_status: (integer, modify) Mechanism specific status code.

set: (Set of Object IDs, modify) The storage associated with the gss_OID_set will be deleted.

Free storage associated with a GSSAPI-generated gss_OID_set object. The set parameter must refer to an OID-set that was returned from a GSS-API routine. gss_release_oid_set() will free the storage associated with each individual member OID, the OID set's elements array, and the gss_OID_set_desc.

The gss_OID_set parameter is set to GSS_C_NO_OID_SET on successful completion of this routine.

Return value:

`GSS_S_COMPLETE`: Successful completion.

gss_create_empty_oid_set

`OM_uint32 gss_create_empty_oid_set` (*OM_uint32* *   [Function]
          `minor_status`, *gss_OID_set* * `oid_set`)

minor_status: (integer, modify) Mechanism specific status code.

oid_set: (Set of Object IDs, modify) The empty object identifier set. The routine will allocate the gss_OID_set_desc object, which the application must free after use with a call to gss_release_oid_set().

Create an object-identifier set containing no object identifiers, to which members may be subsequently added using the gss_add_oid_set_member() routine. These routines are intended to be used to construct sets of mechanism object identifiers, for input to gss_acquire_cred.

Return value:

`GSS_S_COMPLETE`: Successful completion.

gss_test_oid_set_member

`OM_uint32 gss_test_oid_set_member` (*OM_uint32* * `minor_status`,   [Function]
          const gss_OID `member`, *const gss_OID_set* `set`, *int* * `present`)

minor_status: (integer, modify) Mechanism specific status code.

member: (Object ID, read) The object identifier whose presence is to be tested.

set: (Set of Object ID, read) The Object Identifier set.

present: (Boolean, modify) Non-zero if the specified OID is a member of the set, zero if not.

Interrogate an Object Identifier set to determine whether a specified Object Identifier is a member. This routine is intended to be used with OID sets returned by gss_indicate_mechs(), gss_acquire_cred(), and gss_inquire_cred(), but will also work with user-generated sets.

Return value:

`GSS_S_COMPLETE`: Successful completion.

gss_encapsulate_token

extern `OM_uint32 gss_encapsulate_token` (*gss_const_buffer_t*   [Function]
      `input_token`, *gss_const_OID* `token_oid`, *gss_buffer_t* `output_token`)

input_token: (buffer, opaque, read) Buffer with GSS-API context token data.

token_oid: (Object ID, read) Object identifier of token.

output_token: (buffer, opaque, modify) Encapsulated token data; caller must release with gss_release_buffer().

Add the mechanism-independent token header to GSS-API context token data. This is used for the initial token of a GSS-API context establishment sequence. It incorporates an identifier of the mechanism type to be used on that context, and enables tokens to be interpreted unambiguously at GSS-API peers. See further section 3.1 of RFC 2743. This function is standardized in RFC 6339.

Returns:

`GSS_S_COMPLETE`: Indicates successful completion, and that output parameters holds correct information.

`GSS_S_FAILURE`: Indicates that encapsulation failed for reasons unspecified at the GSS-API level.

gss_decapsulate_token

`OM_uint32 gss_decapsulate_token` (*gss_const_buffer_t* `input_token`,   [Function]
      gss_const_OID `token_oid`, *gss_buffer_t* `output_token`)

input_token: (buffer, opaque, read) Buffer with GSS-API context token.

token_oid: (Object ID, read) Expected object identifier of token.

output_token: (buffer, opaque, modify) Decapsulated token data; caller must release with gss_release_buffer().

Remove the mechanism-independent token header from an initial GSS-API context token. Unwrap a buffer in the mechanism-independent token format. This is the reverse of gss_encapsulate_token(). The translation is loss-less, all data is preserved as is. This function is standardized in RFC 6339.

Return value:

`GSS_S_COMPLETE`: Indicates successful completion, and that output parameters holds correct information.

`GSS_S_DEFECTIVE_TOKEN`: Means that the token failed consistency checks (e.g., OID mismatch or ASN.1 DER length errors).

GSS_S_FAILURE: Indicates that decapsulation failed for reasons unspecified at the GSS-API level.

gss_oid_equal

int gss_oid_equal (*gss_const_OID* **first_oid**, *gss_const_OID*   [Function]
        second_oid)

first_oid: (Object ID, read) First Object identifier.

second_oid: (Object ID, read) First Object identifier.

Compare two OIDs for equality. The comparison is "deep", i.e., the actual byte sequences of the OIDs are compared instead of just the pointer equality. This function is standardized in RFC 6339.

Return value: Returns boolean value true when the two OIDs are equal, otherwise false.

3.10 SASL GS2 Routines

gss_inquire_mech_for_saslname

OM_uint32 gss_inquire_mech_for_saslname (*OM_uint32* *   [Function]
        minor_status, *const gss_buffer_t* **sasl_mech_name**, *gss_OID* * **mech_type**)

minor_status: (Integer, modify) Mechanism specific status code.

sasl_mech_name: (buffer, character-string, read) Buffer with SASL mechanism name.

mech_type: (OID, modify, optional) Actual mechanism used. The OID returned via this parameter will be a pointer to static storage that should be treated as read-only; In particular the application should not attempt to free it. Specify NULL if not required.

Output GSS-API mechanism OID of mechanism associated with given @sasl_mech_name.

Returns:

GSS_S_COMPLETE: Successful completion.

GSS_S_BAD_MECH: There is no GSS-API mechanism known as @sasl_mech_name.

gss_inquire_saslname_for_mech

OM_uint32 gss_inquire_saslname_for_mech (*OM_uint32* *   [Function]
        minor_status, *const gss_OID* **desired_mech**, *gss_buffer_t*
        sasl_mech_name, *gss_buffer_t* **mech_name**, *gss_buffer_t* **mech_description**)

minor_status: (Integer, modify) Mechanism specific status code.

desired_mech: (OID, read) Identifies the GSS-API mechanism to query.

sasl_mech_name: (buffer, character-string, modify, optional) Buffer to receive SASL mechanism name. The application must free storage associated with this name after use with a call to gss_release_buffer().

mech_name: (buffer, character-string, modify, optional) Buffer to receive human readable mechanism name. The application must free storage associated with this name after use with a call to gss_release_buffer().

mech_description: (buffer, character-string, modify, optional) Buffer to receive description of mechanism. The application must free storage associated with this name after use with a call to gss_release_buffer().

Output the SASL mechanism name of a GSS-API mechanism. It also returns a name and description of the mechanism in a user friendly form.

Returns:

`GSS_S_COMPLETE`: Successful completion.

`GSS_S_BAD_MECH`: The @desired_mech OID is unsupported.

4 Extended GSS API

None of the following functions are standard GSS API functions. As such, they are not declared in **gss/api.h**, but rather in **gss/ext.h** (which is included from **gss.h**). See Section 2.1 [Header], page 7.

gss_check_version

const char * gss_check_version (*const char * req_version*)　　　　[Function]
　　req_version: version string to compare with, or NULL

　　Check that the version of the library is at minimum the one given as a string in @req_version.

　　Return value: The actual version string of the library; NULL if the condition is not met. If NULL is passed to this function no check is done and only the version string is returned.

gss_userok

int gss_userok (*const gss_name_t* **name**, *const char * **username**)　　　　[Function]
　　name: (gss_name_t, read) Name to be compared.

　　username: Zero terminated string with username.

　　Compare the username against the output from gss_export_name() invoked on @name, after removing the leading OID. This answers the question whether the particular mechanism would authenticate them as the same principal

　　Return value: Returns 0 if the names match, non-0 otherwise.

5 Invoking gss

Name

GNU GSS (gss) – Command line interface to the GSS Library.

Description

gss is the main program of GNU GSS.

Mandatory or optional arguments to long options are also mandatory or optional for any corresponding short options.

Commands

gss recognizes these commands:

```
-l, --list-mechanisms
                    List information about supported mechanisms
                    in a human readable format.
-m, --major=LONG   Describe a 'major status' error code value.
-a, --accept-sec-context
                    Accept a security context as server.
-i, --init-sec-context=MECH
                    Initialize a security context as client.
                    MECH is the SASL name of mechanism, use -l
                    to list supported mechanisms.
-n, --server-name=SERVICE@HOSTNAME
                    For -i, set the name of the remote host.
                    For example, "imap@mail.example.com".
```

Other Options

These are some standard parameters.

```
-h, --help         Print help and exit
-V, --version      Print version and exit
-q, --quiet        Silent operation  (default=off)
```

Examples

To list the supported mechanisms, use `gss -l` like this:

```
$ src/gss -l
Found 1 supported mechanisms.

Mechanism 0:
        Mechanism name: Kerberos V5
        Mechanism description: Kerberos V5 GSS-API mechanism
        SASL Mechanism name: GS2-KRB5
$
```

To initialize a Kerberos V5 security context, use the `--init-sec-context` parameter. Kerberos V5 needs to know the name of the remote entity, so you need to supply the `--server-name` parameter as well. That will provide the name of the server. For example, use `imap@mail.example.com` to setup a security context with the `imap` service on the host `mail.example.com`. The Kerberos V5 client will use your ticket-granting ticket (which needs to be available) and acquire a server ticket for the service. The KDC must know about the server for this to work. The tool will print the GSS-API context tokens base64 encoded on standard output.

```
$ gss -i GS2-KRB5 -n host@interop.josefsson.org
Context token (protection is available):
YIICIQYJKoZIhvcSAQICAQBuggIQMIICDKADAgEFoQMCAQ6iBwMFACAAAACjggEYYYIBFDCCARCgAwIBBaEXGxVpbnR
Input context token:
```

The tool is waiting for the final Kerberos V5 context token from the server. Note the status text informing you that message protection is available.

To accept a Kerberos V5 context, the process is similar. The server needs to know its name, so that it can find the host key from (typically) `/etc/shishi/shishi.keys`. Once started it will wait for a context token from the client. Below we'll paste in the token printed above.

```
$ gss -a -n host@interop.josefsson.org
Importing name "host@interop.josefsson.org"...
Acquiring credentials...
Input context token:
YIICIQYJKoZIhvcSAQICAQBuggIQMIICDKADAgEFoQMCAQ6iBwMFACAAAACjggEYYYIBFDCCARCgAwIBBaEXGxVpbnR
Context has been accepted.  Final context token:
YHEGCSqGSIb3EgECAgIAb2IwYKADAgEFoQMCAQ+iVDBSoAMCARKhAwIBAKJGBESy1Zoy9DrG+DuV/6aWmAp79s9d+of
$
```

Returning to the client, you may now cut'n'paste the final context token as shown by the server. The client has then authenticated the server as well. The output from the client is shown below.

```
YHEGCSqGSIb3EgECAgIAb2IwYKADAgEFoQMCAQ+iVDBSoAMCARKhAwIBAKJGBESy1Zoy9DrG+DuV/6aWmAp79s9d+of
Context has been initialized.
$
```

6 Acknowledgements

This manual borrows text from RFC 2743 and RFC 2744 that describe GSS API formally.

Appendix A Criticism of GSS

The author has doubts whether GSS is the best solution for free software projects looking for a implementation agnostic security framework. We express these doubts in this section, so that the reader can judge for herself if any of the potential problems discussed here are relevant for their project, or if the benefit outweigh the problems. We are aware that some of the opinions are highly subjective, but we offer them in the hope they can serve as anecdotal evidence.

GSS can be criticized on several levels. We start with the actual implementation.

GSS does not appear to be designed by experienced C programmers. While generally this may be a good thing (C is not the best language), but since they defined the API in C, it is unfortunate. The primary evidence of this is the major_status and minor_status error code solution. It is a complicated way to describe error conditions, but what makes matters worse, the error condition is separated; half of the error condition is in the function return value and the other half is in the first argument to the function, which is always a pointer to an integer. (The pointer is not even allowed to be NULL, if the application doesn't care about the minor error code.) This makes the API unreadable, and difficult to use. A better solutions would be to return a struct containing the entire error condition, which can be accessed using macros, although we acknowledge that the C language used at the time GSS was designed may not have allowed this (this may in fact be the reason the awkward solution was chosen). Instead, the return value could have been passed back to callers using a pointer to a struct, accessible using various macros, and the function could have a void prototype. The fact that minor_status is placed first in the parameter list increases the pain it is to use the API. Important parameters should be placed first. A better place for minor_status (if it must be present at all) would have been last in the prototypes.

Another evidence of the C inexperience are the memory management issues; GSS provides functions to deallocate data stored within, e.g., `gss_buffer_t` but the caller is responsible of deallocating the structure pointed at by the `gss_buffer_t` (i.e., the `gss_buffer_desc`) itself. Memory management issues are error prone, and this division easily leads to memory leaks (or worse). Instead, the API should be the sole owner of all `gss_ctx_id_t`, `gss_cred_id_t`, and `gss_buffer_t` structures: they should be allocated by the library, and deallocated (using the utility functions defined for this purpose) by the library.

TBA: specification is unclear how memory for OIDs are managed. For example, who is responsible for deallocate potentially newly allocated OIDs returned as `actual_mechs` in `gss_acquire_cred`? Further, are OIDs deeply copied into OID sets? In other words, if I add an OID into an OID set, and modify the original OID, will the OID in the OID set be modified too?

Another illustrating example is the sample GSS header file given in the RFC, which contains:

```
/*
 * We have included the xom.h header file.  Verify that OM_uint32
 * is defined correctly.
 */
#if sizeof(gss_uint32) != sizeof(OM_uint32)
#error Incompatible definition of OM_uint32 from xom.h
```

```
#endif
```

The C pre-processor does not know about the `sizeof` function, so it is treated as an identifier, which maps to 0. Thus, the expression does not check that the size of `OM_uint32` is correct. It checks whether the expression 0 != 0 holds.

TBA: thread issues

TBA: multiple mechanisms in a GSS library

TBA: high-level design criticism.

TBA: no credential forwarding.

TBA: internationalization

TBA: dynamically generated OIDs and memory deallocation issue. I.e., should gss_import_name or gss_duplicate_name allocate memory and copy the OID provided, or simply copy the pointer? If the former, who would deallocate that memory? If the latter, the application may deallocate or modify the OID, which seem unwanted.

TBA: krb5: no way to access authorization-data

TBA: krb5: firewall/pre-IP: iakerb status?

TBA: krb5: single-DES only

TBA: the API may block, unusable in select() based servers. Especially if the servers contacted is decided by the, yet unauthenticated, remote client.

TBA: krb5: no support for GSS_C_PROT_READY_FLAG. We support it anyway, though.

TBA: krb5: gssapi-cfx differ from rfc 1964 in the reply token in that the latter require presence of sequence numbers whereas the former doesn't.

Finally we note that few free security applications uses GSS, perhaps the only major exception to this are Kerberos 5 implementations. While not substantial evidence, this do suggest that the GSS may not be the simplest solution available to solve actual problems, since otherwise more projects would have chosen to take advantage of the work that went into GSS instead of using another framework (or designing their own solution).

Our conclusion is that free software projects that are looking for a security framework should evaluate carefully whether GSS actually is the best solution before using it. In particular it is recommended to compare GSS with the Simple Authentication and Security Layer (SASL) framework, which in several situations provide the same feature as GSS does. The most compelling argument for SASL over GSS is, as its acronym suggest, Simple, whereas GSS is far from it.

However, that said, for free software projects that wants to support Kerberos 5, we do acknowledge that no other framework provides a more portable and interoperable interface into the Kerberos 5 system. If your project needs to use Kerberos 5 specifically, we do recommend you to use GSS instead of the Kerberos 5 implementation specific APIs.

Appendix B Copying Information

B.1 GNU Free Documentation License

Version 1.3, 3 November 2008

Copyright © 2000, 2001, 2002, 2007, 2008 Free Software Foundation, Inc.
`http://fsf.org/`

Everyone is permitted to copy and distribute verbatim copies
of this license document, but changing it is not allowed.

0. PREAMBLE

The purpose of this License is to make a manual, textbook, or other functional and useful document *free* in the sense of freedom: to assure everyone the effective freedom to copy and redistribute it, with or without modifying it, either commercially or non-commercially. Secondarily, this License preserves for the author and publisher a way to get credit for their work, while not being considered responsible for modifications made by others.

This License is a kind of "copyleft", which means that derivative works of the document must themselves be free in the same sense. It complements the GNU General Public License, which is a copyleft license designed for free software.

We have designed this License in order to use it for manuals for free software, because free software needs free documentation: a free program should come with manuals providing the same freedoms that the software does. But this License is not limited to software manuals; it can be used for any textual work, regardless of subject matter or whether it is published as a printed book. We recommend this License principally for works whose purpose is instruction or reference.

1. APPLICABILITY AND DEFINITIONS

This License applies to any manual or other work, in any medium, that contains a notice placed by the copyright holder saying it can be distributed under the terms of this License. Such a notice grants a world-wide, royalty-free license, unlimited in duration, to use that work under the conditions stated herein. The "Document", below, refers to any such manual or work. Any member of the public is a licensee, and is addressed as "you". You accept the license if you copy, modify or distribute the work in a way requiring permission under copyright law.

A "Modified Version" of the Document means any work containing the Document or a portion of it, either copied verbatim, or with modifications and/or translated into another language.

A "Secondary Section" is a named appendix or a front-matter section of the Document that deals exclusively with the relationship of the publishers or authors of the Document to the Document's overall subject (or to related matters) and contains nothing that could fall directly within that overall subject. (Thus, if the Document is in part a textbook of mathematics, a Secondary Section may not explain any mathematics.) The relationship could be a matter of historical connection with the subject or with related matters, or of legal, commercial, philosophical, ethical or political position regarding them.

The "Invariant Sections" are certain Secondary Sections whose titles are designated, as being those of Invariant Sections, in the notice that says that the Document is released under this License. If a section does not fit the above definition of Secondary then it is not allowed to be designated as Invariant. The Document may contain zero Invariant Sections. If the Document does not identify any Invariant Sections then there are none.

The "Cover Texts" are certain short passages of text that are listed, as Front-Cover Texts or Back-Cover Texts, in the notice that says that the Document is released under this License. A Front-Cover Text may be at most 5 words, and a Back-Cover Text may be at most 25 words.

A "Transparent" copy of the Document means a machine-readable copy, represented in a format whose specification is available to the general public, that is suitable for revising the document straightforwardly with generic text editors or (for images composed of pixels) generic paint programs or (for drawings) some widely available drawing editor, and that is suitable for input to text formatters or for automatic translation to a variety of formats suitable for input to text formatters. A copy made in an otherwise Transparent file format whose markup, or absence of markup, has been arranged to thwart or discourage subsequent modification by readers is not Transparent. An image format is not Transparent if used for any substantial amount of text. A copy that is not "Transparent" is called "Opaque".

Examples of suitable formats for Transparent copies include plain ASCII without markup, Texinfo input format, LaTeX input format, SGML or XML using a publicly available DTD, and standard-conforming simple HTML, PostScript or PDF designed for human modification. Examples of transparent image formats include PNG, XCF and JPG. Opaque formats include proprietary formats that can be read and edited only by proprietary word processors, SGML or XML for which the DTD and/or processing tools are not generally available, and the machine-generated HTML, PostScript or PDF produced by some word processors for output purposes only.

The "Title Page" means, for a printed book, the title page itself, plus such following pages as are needed to hold, legibly, the material this License requires to appear in the title page. For works in formats which do not have any title page as such, "Title Page" means the text near the most prominent appearance of the work's title, preceding the beginning of the body of the text.

The "publisher" means any person or entity that distributes copies of the Document to the public.

A section "Entitled XYZ" means a named subunit of the Document whose title either is precisely XYZ or contains XYZ in parentheses following text that translates XYZ in another language. (Here XYZ stands for a specific section name mentioned below, such as "Acknowledgements", "Dedications", "Endorsements", or "History".) To "Preserve the Title" of such a section when you modify the Document means that it remains a section "Entitled XYZ" according to this definition.

The Document may include Warranty Disclaimers next to the notice which states that this License applies to the Document. These Warranty Disclaimers are considered to be included by reference in this License, but only as regards disclaiming warranties: any other implication that these Warranty Disclaimers may have is void and has no effect on the meaning of this License.

2. VERBATIM COPYING

You may copy and distribute the Document in any medium, either commercially or noncommercially, provided that this License, the copyright notices, and the license notice saying this License applies to the Document are reproduced in all copies, and that you add no other conditions whatsoever to those of this License. You may not use technical measures to obstruct or control the reading or further copying of the copies you make or distribute. However, you may accept compensation in exchange for copies. If you distribute a large enough number of copies you must also follow the conditions in section 3.

You may also lend copies, under the same conditions stated above, and you may publicly display copies.

3. COPYING IN QUANTITY

If you publish printed copies (or copies in media that commonly have printed covers) of the Document, numbering more than 100, and the Document's license notice requires Cover Texts, you must enclose the copies in covers that carry, clearly and legibly, all these Cover Texts: Front-Cover Texts on the front cover, and Back-Cover Texts on the back cover. Both covers must also clearly and legibly identify you as the publisher of these copies. The front cover must present the full title with all words of the title equally prominent and visible. You may add other material on the covers in addition. Copying with changes limited to the covers, as long as they preserve the title of the Document and satisfy these conditions, can be treated as verbatim copying in other respects.

If the required texts for either cover are too voluminous to fit legibly, you should put the first ones listed (as many as fit reasonably) on the actual cover, and continue the rest onto adjacent pages.

If you publish or distribute Opaque copies of the Document numbering more than 100, you must either include a machine-readable Transparent copy along with each Opaque copy, or state in or with each Opaque copy a computer-network location from which the general network-using public has access to download using public-standard network protocols a complete Transparent copy of the Document, free of added material. If you use the latter option, you must take reasonably prudent steps, when you begin distribution of Opaque copies in quantity, to ensure that this Transparent copy will remain thus accessible at the stated location until at least one year after the last time you distribute an Opaque copy (directly or through your agents or retailers) of that edition to the public.

It is requested, but not required, that you contact the authors of the Document well before redistributing any large number of copies, to give them a chance to provide you with an updated version of the Document.

4. MODIFICATIONS

You may copy and distribute a Modified Version of the Document under the conditions of sections 2 and 3 above, provided that you release the Modified Version under precisely this License, with the Modified Version filling the role of the Document, thus licensing distribution and modification of the Modified Version to whoever possesses a copy of it. In addition, you must do these things in the Modified Version:

A. Use in the Title Page (and on the covers, if any) a title distinct from that of the Document, and from those of previous versions (which should, if there were any, be listed in the History section of the Document). You may use the same title as a previous version if the original publisher of that version gives permission.

B. List on the Title Page, as authors, one or more persons or entities responsible for authorship of the modifications in the Modified Version, together with at least five of the principal authors of the Document (all of its principal authors, if it has fewer than five), unless they release you from this requirement.

C. State on the Title page the name of the publisher of the Modified Version, as the publisher.

D. Preserve all the copyright notices of the Document.

E. Add an appropriate copyright notice for your modifications adjacent to the other copyright notices.

F. Include, immediately after the copyright notices, a license notice giving the public permission to use the Modified Version under the terms of this License, in the form shown in the Addendum below.

G. Preserve in that license notice the full lists of Invariant Sections and required Cover Texts given in the Document's license notice.

H. Include an unaltered copy of this License.

I. Preserve the section Entitled "History", Preserve its Title, and add to it an item stating at least the title, year, new authors, and publisher of the Modified Version as given on the Title Page. If there is no section Entitled "History" in the Document, create one stating the title, year, authors, and publisher of the Document as given on its Title Page, then add an item describing the Modified Version as stated in the previous sentence.

J. Preserve the network location, if any, given in the Document for public access to a Transparent copy of the Document, and likewise the network locations given in the Document for previous versions it was based on. These may be placed in the "History" section. You may omit a network location for a work that was published at least four years before the Document itself, or if the original publisher of the version it refers to gives permission.

K. For any section Entitled "Acknowledgements" or "Dedications", Preserve the Title of the section, and preserve in the section all the substance and tone of each of the contributor acknowledgements and/or dedications given therein.

L. Preserve all the Invariant Sections of the Document, unaltered in their text and in their titles. Section numbers or the equivalent are not considered part of the section titles.

M. Delete any section Entitled "Endorsements". Such a section may not be included in the Modified Version.

N. Do not retitle any existing section to be Entitled "Endorsements" or to conflict in title with any Invariant Section.

O. Preserve any Warranty Disclaimers.

If the Modified Version includes new front-matter sections or appendices that qualify as Secondary Sections and contain no material copied from the Document, you may at your option designate some or all of these sections as invariant. To do this, add their titles to the list of Invariant Sections in the Modified Version's license notice. These titles must be distinct from any other section titles.

You may add a section Entitled "Endorsements", provided it contains nothing but endorsements of your Modified Version by various parties—for example, statements of peer review or that the text has been approved by an organization as the authoritative definition of a standard.

You may add a passage of up to five words as a Front-Cover Text, and a passage of up to 25 words as a Back-Cover Text, to the end of the list of Cover Texts in the Modified Version. Only one passage of Front-Cover Text and one of Back-Cover Text may be added by (or through arrangements made by) any one entity. If the Document already includes a cover text for the same cover, previously added by you or by arrangement made by the same entity you are acting on behalf of, you may not add another; but you may replace the old one, on explicit permission from the previous publisher that added the old one.

The author(s) and publisher(s) of the Document do not by this License give permission to use their names for publicity for or to assert or imply endorsement of any Modified Version.

5. COMBINING DOCUMENTS

You may combine the Document with other documents released under this License, under the terms defined in section 4 above for modified versions, provided that you include in the combination all of the Invariant Sections of all of the original documents, unmodified, and list them all as Invariant Sections of your combined work in its license notice, and that you preserve all their Warranty Disclaimers.

The combined work need only contain one copy of this License, and multiple identical Invariant Sections may be replaced with a single copy. If there are multiple Invariant Sections with the same name but different contents, make the title of each such section unique by adding at the end of it, in parentheses, the name of the original author or publisher of that section if known, or else a unique number. Make the same adjustment to the section titles in the list of Invariant Sections in the license notice of the combined work.

In the combination, you must combine any sections Entitled "History" in the various original documents, forming one section Entitled "History"; likewise combine any sections Entitled "Acknowledgements", and any sections Entitled "Dedications". You must delete all sections Entitled "Endorsements."

6. COLLECTIONS OF DOCUMENTS

You may make a collection consisting of the Document and other documents released under this License, and replace the individual copies of this License in the various documents with a single copy that is included in the collection, provided that you follow the rules of this License for verbatim copying of each of the documents in all other respects.

You may extract a single document from such a collection, and distribute it individually under this License, provided you insert a copy of this License into the extracted document, and follow this License in all other respects regarding verbatim copying of that document.

7. AGGREGATION WITH INDEPENDENT WORKS

A compilation of the Document or its derivatives with other separate and independent documents or works, in or on a volume of a storage or distribution medium, is called an "aggregate" if the copyright resulting from the compilation is not used to limit the legal rights of the compilation's users beyond what the individual works permit. When the Document is included in an aggregate, this License does not apply to the other works in the aggregate which are not themselves derivative works of the Document.

If the Cover Text requirement of section 3 is applicable to these copies of the Document, then if the Document is less than one half of the entire aggregate, the Document's Cover Texts may be placed on covers that bracket the Document within the aggregate, or the electronic equivalent of covers if the Document is in electronic form. Otherwise they must appear on printed covers that bracket the whole aggregate.

8. TRANSLATION

Translation is considered a kind of modification, so you may distribute translations of the Document under the terms of section 4. Replacing Invariant Sections with translations requires special permission from their copyright holders, but you may include translations of some or all Invariant Sections in addition to the original versions of these Invariant Sections. You may include a translation of this License, and all the license notices in the Document, and any Warranty Disclaimers, provided that you also include the original English version of this License and the original versions of those notices and disclaimers. In case of a disagreement between the translation and the original version of this License or a notice or disclaimer, the original version will prevail.

If a section in the Document is Entitled "Acknowledgements", "Dedications", or "History", the requirement (section 4) to Preserve its Title (section 1) will typically require changing the actual title.

9. TERMINATION

You may not copy, modify, sublicense, or distribute the Document except as expressly provided under this License. Any attempt otherwise to copy, modify, sublicense, or distribute it is void, and will automatically terminate your rights under this License.

However, if you cease all violation of this License, then your license from a particular copyright holder is reinstated (a) provisionally, unless and until the copyright holder explicitly and finally terminates your license, and (b) permanently, if the copyright holder fails to notify you of the violation by some reasonable means prior to 60 days after the cessation.

Moreover, your license from a particular copyright holder is reinstated permanently if the copyright holder notifies you of the violation by some reasonable means, this is the first time you have received notice of violation of this License (for any work) from that copyright holder, and you cure the violation prior to 30 days after your receipt of the notice.

Termination of your rights under this section does not terminate the licenses of parties who have received copies or rights from you under this License. If your rights have been terminated and not permanently reinstated, receipt of a copy of some or all of the same material does not give you any rights to use it.

10. FUTURE REVISIONS OF THIS LICENSE

The Free Software Foundation may publish new, revised versions of the GNU Free Documentation License from time to time. Such new versions will be similar in spirit to the present version, but may differ in detail to address new problems or concerns. See http://www.gnu.org/copyleft/.

Each version of the License is given a distinguishing version number. If the Document specifies that a particular numbered version of this License "or any later version" applies to it, you have the option of following the terms and conditions either of that specified version or of any later version that has been published (not as a draft) by the Free Software Foundation. If the Document does not specify a version number of this License, you may choose any version ever published (not as a draft) by the Free Software Foundation. If the Document specifies that a proxy can decide which future versions of this License can be used, that proxy's public statement of acceptance of a version permanently authorizes you to choose that version for the Document.

11. RELICENSING

"Massive Multiauthor Collaboration Site" (or "MMC Site") means any World Wide Web server that publishes copyrightable works and also provides prominent facilities for anybody to edit those works. A public wiki that anybody can edit is an example of such a server. A "Massive Multiauthor Collaboration" (or "MMC") contained in the site means any set of copyrightable works thus published on the MMC site.

"CC-BY-SA" means the Creative Commons Attribution-Share Alike 3.0 license published by Creative Commons Corporation, a not-for-profit corporation with a principal place of business in San Francisco, California, as well as future copyleft versions of that license published by that same organization.

"Incorporate" means to publish or republish a Document, in whole or in part, as part of another Document.

An MMC is "eligible for relicensing" if it is licensed under this License, and if all works that were first published under this License somewhere other than this MMC, and subsequently incorporated in whole or in part into the MMC, (1) had no cover texts or invariant sections, and (2) were thus incorporated prior to November 1, 2008.

The operator of an MMC Site may republish an MMC contained in the site under CC-BY-SA on the same site at any time before August 1, 2009, provided the MMC is eligible for relicensing.

ADDENDUM: How to use this License for your documents

To use this License in a document you have written, include a copy of the License in the document and put the following copyright and license notices just after the title page:

```
Copyright (C)  year  your name.
Permission is granted to copy, distribute and/or modify this document
under the terms of the GNU Free Documentation License, Version 1.3
or any later version published by the Free Software Foundation;
with no Invariant Sections, no Front-Cover Texts, and no Back-Cover
Texts.  A copy of the license is included in the section entitled ``GNU
Free Documentation License''.
```

If you have Invariant Sections, Front-Cover Texts and Back-Cover Texts, replace the "with...Texts." line with this:

```
with the Invariant Sections being list their titles, with
the Front-Cover Texts being list, and with the Back-Cover Texts
being list.
```

If you have Invariant Sections without Cover Texts, or some other combination of the three, merge those two alternatives to suit the situation.

If your document contains nontrivial examples of program code, we recommend releasing these examples in parallel under your choice of free software license, such as the GNU General Public License, to permit their use in free software.

Concept Index

API Index

www.ingramcontent.com/pod-product-compliance
Lightning Source LLC
LaVergne TN
LVHW060147070326

832902LV00018B/2997